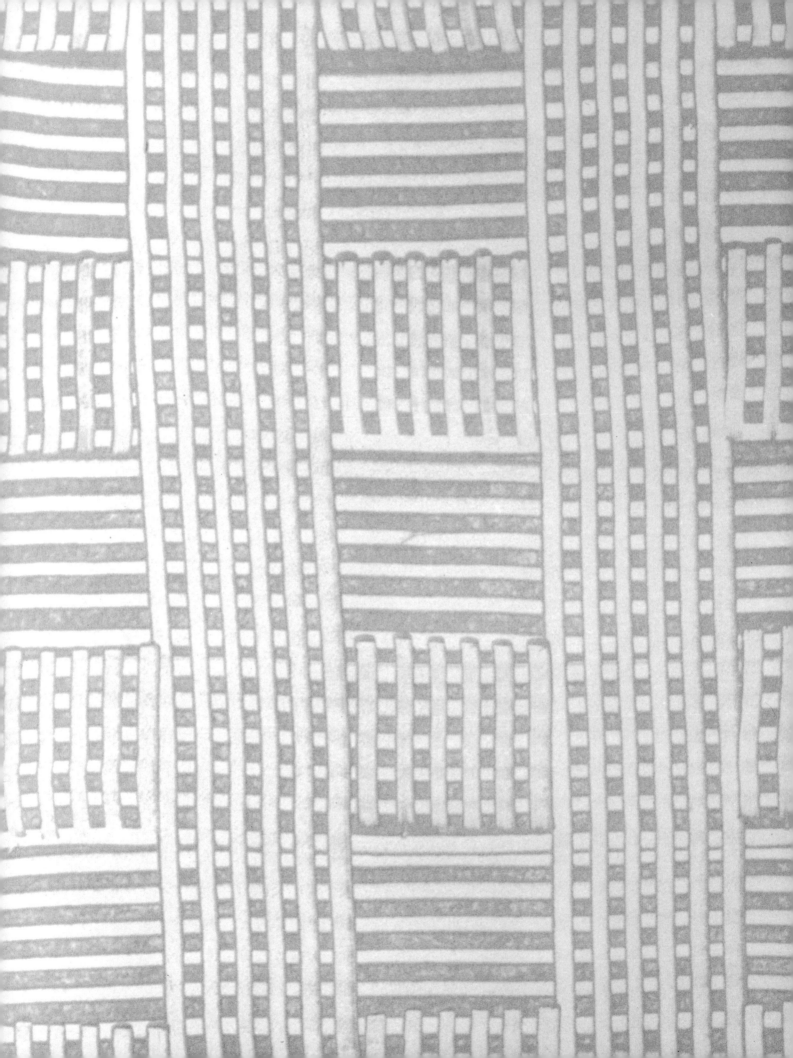

Debbie Travis' Painted House

QUICK AND EASY PAINTED FINISHES FOR WALLS, FLOORS, AND

Debbie Travis' Painted House

DEBBIE TRAVIS

with **BARBARA DINGLE**

FURNITURE USING WATER-BASED PAINTS

Clarkson Potter/Publishers
New York

Copyright © 1997 by Debbie Travis

Principal photography by Ernst Hellrung; additional photography by: Stephane Poulin; Alain Sirois; Richard Poissant; Nicole Khoury; Jean-Luc Laporté; and Christian Guay

Published by Clarkson N. Potter/Publishers, 201 East 50th Street, New York, New York 10022. Member of the Crown Publishing Group.

Random House, Inc. New York, Toronto, London, Sydney, Auckland

http://www.randomhouse.com/

CLARKSON N. POTTER, POTTER, and colophon are trademarks of Clarkson N. Potter, Inc.

DEBBIE TRAVIS' PAINTED HOUSE and the paintbrush logo are trademarks of Whalley-Abbey Media Holdings, Inc.

Printed in China

DESIGN BY LISA GOLDENBERG

Library of Congress Cataloging-in-Publication Data
Travis, Debbie.
Debbie Travis' painted house : Quick and easy painted finishes for walls, floors, and furniture using water-based paints / by Debbie Travis ; text by Barbara Dingle.
p. cm.
Includes index.
1. House painting—Amateurs' manuals. 2. Furniture painting—Amateurs' manuals.
3. Interior decoration—Amateurs' manuals. I. Dingle, Barbara. II. Title.
TT323.T73 1997 698'.1—dc21 96-37440 CIP

ISBN 0-609-60155-5

10 9 8 7 6

To the three males in my life
Hans, Josh, and Max—
Hans, who made everything possible,
and Josh and Max for their love
and understanding when my head
was elsewhere.

Acknowledgments

Debbie Travis' Painted House was written because of the enormous response to and success of the *Debbie Travis' Painted House* television series. The many inquiries from viewers seemed to point out the existence of a large demand for a decorative paint book that was packed with innovative ideas and basic, easy-to-follow instructions. It is thanks to the imagination and talent of the team of painters who work on the show that this book was made possible. Huge thanks to Alison Osborn, Debs Brennan, Pauline St. Amand, Elaine Miller, Valerie Finney, Bruce Emo, and Mal McSpurren, and to Caroline Guay for her endless efficiency.

Many thanks to Barbara Dingle, who managed to put all my thoughts, vision, and vivid imagination onto the written page.

I'd like to give particular acknowledgment to my editor at Clarkson Potter, Pam Krauss, for her faith and enthusiasm for this book. Also a special thanks to her dynamic assistant, Margot Schupf.

Special thanks to everyone at my first network, WTN, for all their support. Special thanks also to Maggie Drew at Canadian Manda, who was instrumental in putting the project in motion.

Contents

Part Three Finishes for Furniture, Trim, and Accessories 139

Preface

I have always loved decorating. I remember as a girl constantly rearranging my tiny bedroom, trying to find ingenious ways to make it look either bigger, brighter, cozier, or wilder, depending on my mood. Luckily, I had a mother who gave me free rein with leftover paint, crayons, and wallpaper, provided I kept my efforts within the four walls of my bedroom.

That room would become a canvas for years of experimentation—some projects successful, some better forgotten. I once became obsessed with a picture of a red room I'd seen in a book, and the following weekend spent two weeks' saved pocket money on a gallon of fire-engine red high-gloss paint. On Sunday afternoon, when the whole family had gone for a walk, I gave the walls two coats, and by the time they came back, my room looked like one of the old English phone booths. After suffering constant headaches and finding it hard to study or sleep at night I painted over it. To this day, a pink glow shows through whatever color is on the walls.

Throughout my teens, it wasn't the fashion magazines flaunting the latest skirt length or haircut that set my heart racing, it was shelter (home style) magazines featuring the newest design trends. Soon the confines of my room left me hungry for more expansive spaces to conquer.

At nineteen I struck out on my own and moved into a slightly grim basement apartment. Although I barely had enough money to cover food and rent, I soon discovered that with a little paint, scavenged second-hand furniture, and lots of imagination, I could easily turn those drab rooms into a real home full of color and character.

I'll never forget the exhilaration when my first roommate and I literally stumbled onto our first paint effect. We had painted our living room a pale yellow, and proudly showed it to our friends, who all exclaimed it looked like a room full of scrambled eggs. Thoroughly disheartened, we decided to repaint the room. We chose a dark ochre and rolled on a coat, but when we stood back, we decided the room looked too dark. Grabbing sheets of newspaper, we tried to remove the wet paint. To our great surprise, a wonderful soft, creased effect emerged. We discovered that when we laid the paper flat on the painted surface and pulled it off, the wall looked like suede. We finished the room with squeals of delight, and I've used this effect in other people's living rooms ever since. Of course I now know that it's called frottage, which comes from *frotter,* "to rub" in French (see page 76).

In those early years I learned two important lessons that still hold true today: First, that paint is the most inexpensive decorating tool around, and, second, that it has the power to transform any space into your own personal vision.

Although I studied fine arts, my most valuable experience came from some of the great decorative painters whom I worked alongside in London. They taught me about the beauty of color and the versatility of working with glazes, but most of all I learned not to be afraid to experiment and to develop my own recipes and style. These are the most important lessons I hope to pass along to you.

When I married and moved to Canada in 1986, the art of decorative painting was just beginning to see a resurgence in North America. There were only a few books or how-to magazines on the market. As my career as a decorative painter blossomed, I made up many of my own techniques and tried to simplify some of the complicated recipes I'd previously worked with in England. After teaching paint finishes for several years, I produced four decorative painting videos. These were a great success, and the public demand for simple instructions on versatile, durable painted finishes kept growing, which led to my television series, *Debbie Travis' Painted House.* Now, it seems that everybody has caught paint fever!

As a result of my experiences teaching painting techniques, demonstrating and speaking at home shows, and answering questions on call-in talk shows, I feel my job has evolved from simply teaching people how to paint to also reassuring and persuading them that *anyone* can paint and decorate a room. The actual painted finishes are not what intimidates people, it's getting started that's the trick. Over and over I am asked: How do I choose my colors? How much skill is necessary to achieve these effects? Can I paint over wallpaper, or laminated kitchen cabinets?

This book will answer these questions and more. It is the guide I wish *I'd* had when I first started decorative painting—with lots of pictures to inspire you, and clear, step-by-step instructions to guide you through each painted finish.

The rooms I've selected demonstrate beautifully how simple paint effects can transform plain walls, floors, and furniture. Some books put a degree-of-difficulty marking alongside each paint effect, but I honestly believe that once you learn the basic rules for making a glaze and begin to manipulate and play with paint, all the finishes are easy—and very rewarding.

I am constantly learning and discovering new ways to decorate with paint. I hope that once you get started, you'll use this wonderful decorating medium to fill your home full of your own personality and spirit. And never let a few "miscalculations" like a fire-engine red bedroom or a scrambled egg living room stop you. Don't miss the fun and exhilaration of transforming the rooms you live in every day into spaces that make you smile.

Debbie Travis

PART ONE

Getting Started

Painted finishes are truly impressive—and they always look as if they are a lot more work than they really are! I think that's what stops so many people from painting or decorating their homes themselves. How many times have you said, "Oh, I could never do that, I'm not artistic" or "I don't have the time." Believe me, anyone can paint a room. And armed with a little practice and know-how, anyone can produce stunning paint effects.

This first section of *Debbie Travis' Painted House* is designed to provide you with all the information you need to begin creating beautiful painted effects. It contains invaluable advice on everything from where to find ideas for different projects to choosing the right colors for your home, from how to prime a floor to the correct way to paint a chair. The real key to successful paint finishes is learning a bit about paint so you understand how paints and glazes work. In this book I have concentrated on water-based paints—you may know them as latex and acrylic paints. I find water-based paints to be ideal for indoor projects because they are nearly odorless, dry quickly, and clean up easily off brushes and hands with warm water. If you're truly a beginner, I recommend taking a little time to get used to the feeling of working with a paintbrush, how much paint to pick up at one time, how to work with a roller so that your strokes are smooth. It's important to familiarize yourself with any new paint, glaze, or tool before you begin a large project; you'll be more relaxed and able to enjoy the experience if you feel confident with your equipment.

Long reserved for walls and exteriors only, paint is enjoying a newfound freedom from traditional decorating rules. Don't be afraid to experiment with paint everywhere—after all, walls, floors, and furniture are only surfaces that can be wiped clean, or recovered with another coat of paint or a different finish. And don't lose heart if the final project doesn't measure up to the picture you fell in love with in a book or magazine. Remember, the most successful decorating projects are those you've done yourself, because you've chosen the colors and finishes you love and combined them with personal belongings to create an environment that's uniquely yours. So let's get started!

Finding Inspiration

I'm often asked where I get all the great ideas featured on my television series. I work with an energetic and enthusiastic team who are as taken as I am by the end-

less possibilities and creative solutions that paint offers the home decorator, and here I've included a selection of the resources that often provide us with a starting point whenever we're facing a set of blank walls.

One of my favorites is a scrapbook that contains swatches of fabrics, photos, and other bits and pieces I've collected over the years. Why not make one of your own—it needn't be as elaborate as the one pictured here, and can include any pattern or color that catches your eye, in any form. Remember, personal taste and imagination are the only dictates that count when it comes to decorating your home, and, with a bit of paint, you can create any style you want, on any budget. Here's where to look for ideas:

BOOKS AND MAGAZINES

Wherever you live, there's sure to be an abundance of decorating books and style magazines available, which are always chock full of ideas and advice on how to create the room of your dreams. You'll probably find that you are repeatedly drawn to certain colors, patterns, and themes. Keep track of your favorites by starting a file or scrapbook of rooms and ideas that delight you; it's easy to tear out or photocopy a page of rooms you love. Also, look for the do-it-yourself projects and workshops in these publications. Their step-by-step instructions are another great resource; even if you don't want to recreate one of the featured looks exactly, the information will no doubt prove invaluable for future projects.

These pages from my scrapbook contain swatches of fabric, photographs, and samples of paint finishes and colors—above, around a Swedish theme; opposite, in a garden room vein.

HOME SHOWS

With more and more people now participating in their own home's renovation, many towns and cities now hold annual home shows which showcase new products and decorating ideas. These shows often offer free do-it-yourself workshops, and there are always plenty of demonstrations. If you go, you're likely to meet people who have the same questions as you, and it's always fun to hear about what someone else did with his tiny bathroom, odd-shaped kitchens, or cathedral ceiling. I always walk away with a new idea or two—even when I'm the speaker.

PUBLIC SPACES AND PRIVATE HOMES

Always keep your mind and eyes open when visiting friends' homes and public places such as theaters, shops, restaurants, and even museums—there's an idea to be found around every corner. For example, because restaurants like to keep up with the times, they change their decor frequently, and offer a wealth of contemporary design inspirations. Of course, many themes may be too dramatic for your home, but you can learn a lot by noticing the fundamental ways the designer sets the mood; pay attention to the lighting or the color scheme in addition to the food.

There's no harm in copying decorating ideas when it comes to paint, because paint finishes will always look unique to your home. Even if your friend has ragged her living room walls in yellow, your raspberry-ragged bedroom will have a character all its own.

TELEVISION

Many decorating and lifestyle shows on television, such as *Debbie Travis' Painted House,* walk you through the process of pulling a room together. These shows are packed with ideas and projects for every home decorator, and the projects are usually accompanied by step-by-step instructions. So, set your VCR to tape your favorite shows and add these to your idea library.

Decades of Style

Another place to turn for inspiration is to your home itself. Most homes can be cate-gorized as a type of architectural design simply by their age. If we're lucky, some of our homes date back hundreds of years, but the majority of us probably live in houses or apartments that were built from the Victorian era through the present day. The age of your house, its style, the rooms' physical dimensions, the height of the walls, the slope of the ceilings—all these features can act as decorating cues to help to get you started.

Victorian homes offer superb architectural detailing. Walls often reach ten to twelve feet in height, and are usually adorned with deep plaster moldings, carved window and door trim, and high baseboards. Most interior doors are solid, with carved panels. If you have the patience, you may wish to strip some of the fine wood down to its former beauty. But keep in mind that these features all look spectacular with a simple, fresh coat of white paint. Further embellishment is unnecessary, as the ornate plasterwork and carved wood speak for themselves.

In these older homes, the plaster walls will no doubt be in less than perfect condition and lend themselves beautifully to textured paint finishes such as colorwashing, ragging, and fresco, all finishes that easily disguise an uneven surface. You can even play up the inevitable cracks and repairs with a distressed plaster painted effect. And because Victorian homes have such high ceilings, you can also do interesting things to enliven a large expanse of wall space. Dadoes or chair rails break up the height of the walls, bringing them down to "human" scale. Here's a wonderful

In this Victorian home, the moldings and staircase have been highlighted with a Gothic stencil.

opportunity to play with color and different paint finishes on the upper and lower wall. **Houses from the thirties and forties** offer a scaled-down version of the architectural features found in century-old homes. Walls are not quite so high, and the moldings, while still present, are simpler. The doors, trim, and moldings in these rooms look magnificent with faux finishes such as marble and tortoiseshell, but can look just as good with a simple dragged finish. If the trim is wood, as is often the case in homes of this period,

leave it as is, and highlight only the walls.

The walls will often have layers of wallpaper that have already been painted over once or twice. Stripping away the paper will no doubt expose damaged plaster, which will need some work to repair. To save time you can simply apply a couple of coats of paint. The texture of the wallpaper will add depth and character to the finish. There is most likely a lovely hardwood floor under all that wall-to-wall carpeting. The grain of the wood will come up beautifully with an interesting stain or paint design.

Mass-market building from the fifties to the seventies introduced a cheaper, no-frills interior to houses. Ceilings dropped, moldings disappeared, window and door trim, as well as baseboards, became purely utilitarian in form. In these rather plain interiors, the trick is to draw the eye away from awkward or uninteresting features. Paint low ceilings white—a dark color will only press down on the room, giving you the feeling you're inside a box. Diminish the visibility of boring trims by painting them the same color as the walls. In these homes, instead of plaster, the walls are some form of wallboard (gyproc or drywall), the perfect canvas for all the spectacular paint finishes that demand a smooth surface. Such rooms cry out for an exciting paint technique such as stripes or combing, which are inappropriate for a plaster wall, where the cracks and bumps would stand out and spoil the finish.

Stencils are an easy way to add detail to plain walls.

If your walls have few moldings, then stencils are an easy way to add detail. If the ceilings are low, make your floors a feature. An old parquet floor might look dated and yellow, but it makes a perfect grid for an exciting floor finish.

Contemporary construction, in many cases, is dominated by the concept of open indoor living space, where rooms flow together with no physical barriers to separate sitting, dining, and cooking areas. Cathedral ceilings, walls of glass, and a continuous sweep of hardwood floor cre-

ate an airy and refreshing environment. This style also inspires a whole new set of decorating challenges. Where do you start and stop with paint? Must you stick to one finish throughout? One way to break the expanse of a wall that rises two stories is to create a visual break by running borders at a natural ceiling height. You have now divided the space into an upper and lower wall, perfect for complementary finishes and colors.

Another common problem in contemporary spaces concerns the proper way to divide an open-plan living/dining room. Here is a technique I have used with great success: Paint faux panels onto the walls of both "rooms" using three colors from the same color family. Keep the "frame" around the panels the same color throughout. Paint the panels a light shade in the living room and a darker complementary shade in the dining room. The same design and background color keep the space connected, while the change in panel colors gives each space its own character.

Working with a Theme

If you're unsure of the look you want, keep in mind that one of the most interesting ways of designing a room is around a theme. The idea can come from anywhere— a favorite piece of furniture or accessory, a particular color, or a look culled from the pages of a book or magazine.

There is no need to adhere rigidly to any one theme, style, or era of decoration; just as rustic country pieces can mingle gracefully with modern pieces, you may choose to pair an elegant painted finish such as faux tortoiseshell with informal furnishings, or warm up a starkly modern interior with rich medieval tones. Imagine a standard white vestibule in a modern home; even with some pictures and a mirror, it may always look stark and plain. Try stone-blocking the walls in brown, beige, and sandy tones to create a warm, welcoming entrance. Or imagine your bedroom with Southwestern colors and a few cacti, or painted in cool yellow and blue Scandinavian tones with a pretty stencil border.

With the right accessories and the correct colors, even the most ordinary rooms can take on new style and character. And while paint makes a powerful impression, these looks cost little to achieve. On the following pages are rooms that I've built up around a specific theme, inspired by trips abroad, furniture I picked up at flea markets, a few yards of fabric, or a color palette I loved. These rooms are here to give you ideas. It's not necessary to incorporate every finish and accessory listed or pictured here to capture the true spirit of each theme. Use them simply as a guide, and let your imagination do the rest.

SOUTHWESTERN OR DESERT

You don't have to live in the heat of the desert to have its warmth in your home. The look is fun and relaxed, perfect for a den or any casual space, and it's an easy one to pull together—if you have some terra-cotta pots, wrought iron, and comfortable furnishings, you're well on your way. Color is all-important in establishing a Southwestern theme—here, vibrant red, ochre, turquoise, and green punctuate sun-bleached wood and sandy tones. We continued the spirit by adding a Navajo border and stencilled Kokapelles lizards. This den is in a modern home with very little architectural detail; luckily, the floors were wood, an important design element of Southwestern style. The original fireplace surround was brass, however, which didn't fit in very well, so we replaced the brass with wood, and gave it a faded, aged look by colorwashing with some white paint. Like the house itself, the furnishings are modern, but plain. Because the walls were cathedral height, I created my own border with kitchen sponges and a stencil;

COLORS	PAINT FINISHES	ACCESSORIES
SAND	COLORWASHING	TERRA-COTTA POTS
TERRA-COTTA	ANTIQUING/AGING	CACTUS PLANTS
OCHRE	STAMPING	DRIFTWOOD
TURQUOISE	FAUX PLASTER	WROUGHT IRON
DEEP RED	STENCILING	BLEACHED WOOD
	VERDIGRIS	NAVAJO PRINTS, BLANKETS, AND RUGS
		LARGE CANDLES, TALL CANDLESTICKS

this brings the wall a little more into human scale and makes for a cozier den, and by throwing down some Navajo-inspired rugs, this inviting space is complete.

CHEAP AND CHIC

No money, lots of style. Believe it or not, most of the furnishings in this room were found in junkshops and transformed with paint. Decorating on a budget is always a challenge, but let your imagination soar—often the most interesting looks are created by chance using only what's on hand. Almost any paint finish can be used, but instead of choosing traditional shades, go wild and try some unusual colors. This living/dining room was great fun to paint. The mix of colors is unusual but works out well—you just have to be brave; lay out color chips from a paint store and play with combinations until you get the WOW factor. The empty hanging picture frame, a cheap hardware store find covered in inexpensive crushed velvet, helps divide up the space in this large loft. Old fifties cabinet TV sets are easy to find in junkshops, and painted in crazy colors, they make great consoles or end tables. The table is yellow, black and white faux granite (pages 135–137) and the walls are emerald and indigo, with a burgundy border. Incidentally, the walls were colorwashed with a roller, the fastest paint finish you can do (pages 55–57). The overall look is comfortable, yet sophisticated—perfect for casual entertaining.

COLORS	PAINT FINISHES	ACCESSORIES
ANYTHING GOES	COLORWASHING	FLEA MARKET FIXUPS
MIX STRONG COLORS	FAUX GRANITE OR MARBLE	POSTERS, PRINTS
WITH PASTELS	IN FANTASY COLORS	NO-SEW CURTAINS
INDIGO	FREEHAND PAINTING	
BURGUNDY	SPONGING	
YELLOW	RAGGING	
BLACK	BAGGING	
EMERALD	TARTAN	

AFRICAN SAFARI

The inspiration behind this living room was the wonderful textures and colors of Africa. Although I've never had the opportunity to visit, I've always loved reading books and watching TV shows about this great continent. As a background, we've

flogged (see pages 81–83) the walls in a soft grassy green. There were no moldings, so I created my own with a piece of polystyrene foam cut into a comb (see page 107). One or two bright accessories easily enliven this already interesting theme, and now most cities have ethnic stores where you can find beautiful yet inexpensive fabrics and rugs. Baskets, boxes, trunks, cookware, or weapons that are used exclusively for their intended purposes by other cultures can also be used for decoration in your home. Here, spears stand in as curtain rods, and cooking pots make great plant holders. African colors revolve around a palette of beiges, taupes, and browns, and are brought to life with bright greens and earthy reds.

SHABBY CHIC

Combining crisp, clean whites and soft, muted colors with well-worn furnishings is the keynote of this popular theme. The idea is to collect objects in tones of white, mixing good pieces and restored flea market finds and put them together against a pastel backdrop. The look is loose and inviting, with comfy old

COLORS	PAINT FINISHES	ACCESSORIES
GRASS GREEN	COLORWASHING	AFRICAN FABRICS
BEIGE	RAGGING	WOOD FURNITURE,
TAUPE	ANTIQUING	EITHER MAHOGANY
BROWN	FLOGGING	OR TEAK
DARK RED	STUCCO	FAUX ANIMAL SKINS
	CRACKLE FINISH	SPEARS
	STAMPING	BASKETS
	COMBING	LARGE-LEAF PLANTS
		AFRICAN TRINKETS

COLORS	PAINT FINISHES	ACCESSORIES
SHADES OF WHITE, FROM CREAM, BEIGE, GRAY, TO PASTELS, FADED COLORS	COLORWASH RAGGING, DRAGGING FRESCO STUCCO ANTIQUING CRACKLE FINISH STENCILING COLORWASH ON WOOD	SLIPCOVERS BIG SOFT CHAIRS, COUCHES ANTIQUES GARAGE SALE FINDS WARM CARPETS OLD LAMPS

chairs or couches re-covered in off-white textures, accessories in light tones, some lace for a pretty accent and a warm carpet underfoot. When white is lightly tinted with other colors you can create a broad spectrum of "off whites"—literally hundreds of shades, from creams and beiges to pastel whites with a hint of blue, pink or yellow. In this room the pure white on the chair rail and fireplace anchor and frame the room, as well as highlight the beautiful duck egg blue walls, and off-white tones in the furnishings. The old carved coffee table was enlivened with a coat of crackle and white paint, and a new needlepoint carpet was flipped to show the more muted palette underneath. This comfortable style fits every budget—it's broken in enough for the kids and pets, yet chic enough for company.

EASTERN INFLUENCE

This ornate style demands rich color and detailed patterns. Silk cushions and oriental carpets add much to the design, but this is also the perfect setting for a variety of paint finishes such as antiquing and stenciling. Touches of gold can be added everywhere, to lamps,

frames, and furniture. I often find that homeowners are afraid to work with dark colors. There's a myth that the rooms will look smaller. But deep colors add wonderful atmosphere to any room. I've added Asian pieces and accessories which work beautifully with the ragged walls and gold paisley stencils. The walls originally had a textured wallpaper which I left on and painted over,

using a dark red glaze ragged over a lighter red. Dramatic decorating is better suited to rooms we don't "live" in, but creates an exciting setting for entertaining.

COLORS	PAINT FINISHES	ACCESSORIES
JEWEL TONES:	RAGGING	RICH FABRICS TRIMMED
RED	BAGGING	WITH GOLD, TASSELS
SAPPHIRE BLUE	ANTIQUING	ASIAN BOXES, TRUNKS
OCHRE	CRACKLE FINISH	ORNATE MIRRORS AND
GOLD	FROTTAGE	PICTURE FRAMES
	PATINA	
	GILDING	
	STENCILING	

COUNTRY FARMHOUSE

Nowadays, country kitchens are popular in city and suburban homes because of their warmth and comfortable style. The country look is also one of the easiest looks to reproduce, given the right paint colors and accessories. Due to increasing demand, most manufacturers have launched a series of historic paint colors; these low-key, rustic shades make marvelous partners with complementary finishes such as ragging and dragging, or with an aged effect. Of course, these heritage colors also look great on their own.

This is actually a newly built kitchen with inexpensive pine cupboards, but by applying a dragged and ragged effect with historic paint colors, the whole room has a country style. With a couple of coats of varnish applied to the surfaces, this homey kitchen will stand up to everyday wear and tear. Pots hang within easy reach; utensils and crockery double as perfect decorative accents.

COLORS	PAINT FINISHES	ACCESSORIES
RUSTIC NATURALS	RAGGING	PINE HUTCH
OLD GREEN	DRAGGING	CAST-IRON COOKWARE
RUSTY RED	ANTIQUING/AGING	BARRELS
YELLOW OCHRE	COLORWASHING	BASKETS
TEAL BLUE	STENCILING	OLD TOOLS
	STAINING	

COLORS	PAINT FINISHES	ACCESSORIES
A WIDE SPECTRUM OF PASTELS AND RICH DEEP SHADES	SPONGING RAGGING COLORWASHING DRAGGING ANTIQUING VERDIGRIS STAMPING/BLOCK PAINTING STENCILING	ANY TYPE OF COLLECTION BOTANICAL PRINTS ANTIQUES PLATE RAILS LACE, CHINTZ, TARTAN BOOKS FLOWERS

ENGLISH COUNTRY STYLE

It's the furnishings that lend English country style its warm, inviting look. Couches, chairs, tables, and knicknacks, passed along through generations, have a built-in, well-worn comfort to them. Most colors can be used in this style, but don't try to create any sharp contrasts. Layer tablecloths, carpets, and window treatments, and display prints, photographs—anything you collect, wherever there's room. Here, softly textured wall finishes like colorwashes make a perfect backdrop for this pretty, welcome look—it's the soft terra-cotta colors that give this effect. In daylight, this dining room is fresh and sunny, but in the evening, with the right lighting, the room takes on an intimate, romantic glow. The charming wisteria (see pages 177–179) was easy to apply and gives a completely different look than stenciling. This block painting technique works equally as well in a bedroom, bathroom, or kitchen—anywhere you want to add a bit of whimsy or old-fashioned charm.

SCANDINAVIAN INFLUENCE

I've always loved the light-filled interiors of Scandinavian homes. Although the styles vary from Sweden to Norway and from Denmark to Finland, their rooms are generally simple and graceful. Colors are pure and cool, and detail is often naive. The Scandinavians' love for painted finishes goes back centuries, and is especially evident on their furnishings, from simple country pieces to highly decorated armoires,

COLORS	PAINT FINISHES	ACCESSORIES
GRAY BLUES TERRA-COTTA PALE YELLOWS SOFT GREENS WHITE	STENCILING DRAGGING COLORWASHING PAINTED STUCCO FRESCO ANTIQUING CRACKLE FINISH	LOTS OF WOOD FURNITURE WITH SIMPLE LINES COUNTRY ANTIQUES PINE PIECES RUGS

COLORS	PAINT FINISHES	ACCESSORIES

LAVENDER
BLUE
BRIGHT YELLOW
ANY COLORS FOUND
   IN THE GARDEN
	STENCILING
	STAMPING
	COLORWASHING
	RAGGING
	SPONGING
		LOTS OF POTS OF
		   FLOWERS
		WICKER FURNITURE
		HAND-PAINTED
		   FURNITURE
		SISAL RUGS

beds, and bureaus. Here I've chosen a clean, fresh blue and white palette, and set the stage by dragging (see pages 67–69) a blue glaze over a white base coat on the walls. The homemade stencil and crisp linens suit the mood perfectly. Although wall-to-wall carpet is not typically Scandinavian, it was already in this girl's bedroom, and its natural color and fiber work well with this timeless style. It's always important to work with what you have got. This simple yet elegant look will last a long time.

A GARDEN ROOM

Any size or shape room will make a perfect garden room, as long as there are windows large enough to let in lots of natural light. A minimum of decorating is required, as this theme revolves around beautiful rows of potted plants and flowers. Here we started with a pretty round room with wainscoting from floor to ceiling, and I wanted it to be bright and cheerful every day, no matter what the weather. To pick the colors, I just took a look at my garden, and decided on lavender blue and a bright buttercup yellow—nature's palette is a perfect inspiration for any room. The interesting details of the windows were highlighted by painting them lavender, and then applying a reverse stenciled border. I also decorated inexpensive clay pots for my indoor garden, each with a different paint finish; and onto some, I glued natural materials such as moss and raffia, as well as buttons—anything you have on hand will do. This is a good way to practice decorative paint finishes before tackling a room. Even if the pots don't turn out perfect the first time, with plants in them, they'll look great!

MACKINTOSH STYLE

Charles Rennie Mackintosh (1868–1928), one of Scotland's greatest architects and designers, is the inspiration behind this dining room. Inspired by the Arts and Crafts movement, Mackintosh was a great admirer of stencils and stained glass. He loved clean lines and simple shapes, and often turned to nature as a source for decoration. His choice of color was unusual for his time; the Victorians surrounded themselves with a dark, rather morbid palette and busy patterns, whereas Mackintosh chose soft greens, lilac, and his signature black as accents against gray or white walls.

This dining room is my adaptation of the Mackintosh style. The gray walls have been paneled with lilac stripes, but instead of plain paint,

I've softened the room by ragging the stripes. The panels have been decorated with a Mackintosh stencil (see Resources at the end of this book), which has also been used on the window blinds. The black highback chairs are modern pieces based on Mackintosh's designs. To create this look, you need a plain room with few or no moldings. Just combine typical colors, simple stencil patterns, and sleek, unadorned furnishings and it will work wonderfully.

COLORS	PAINT FINISHES	ACCESSORIES
BLACK	STENCILING	MODERN FURNISHINGS
WHITE	RAGGING	STAINED GLASS
GRAY		WINDOW BLINDS
LILAC		ANYTHING LINEAR
PALE GREEN		
ROSE PINK		

Choosing Colors

Another important element of your painted finish is color, which seems to be one of the biggest stumbling blocks for many people. I can't tell you what color to paint your room—a question I'm asked repeatedly—but I can show you what colors work well together, and how you can choose color combinations that will please you.

Don't be afraid to experiment with different colors as well as different finishes when you're decorating; go with colors you love, the way you do when you are shopping for clothes. Bold colors are perfect for rooms in which you entertain; washed-out or faded colors provide soft, subtle backgrounds in busy rooms like kitchens and bathrooms. Bright colors like apple green, primrose yellow, and cornflower blue are perfect for what I call happy rooms, such as dens and children's bedrooms, while darker colors appealingly reflect the differences between day and evening lighting, looking simple and elegant during the day and romantic at night.

I'm always surprised at how many people are afraid of putting color on their walls. "Oh, I'd love to put a dark green in my living room, but I'm afraid it will make the room too small" or "I'll tire of it" are both common laments, and so many stay with beige, cream, or white walls. There's nothing wrong with these colors; on the contrary, a room painted in different tones of white can be quite beautiful. You've no doubt noticed that in all the high-end interior design and architecture magazines the walls are consistently white or beige.

The luxurious furnishings in these rooms speak for themselves; they are the focal point, and the plain white walls serve as a muted background. But most of us don't have priceless antiques, so our rooms can be given character, passion, elegance, and charm by choosing wonderful colors and simple-to-produce painted finishes.

COLOR AT YOUR FINGERTIPS

You don't have to know how to mix colors to work with all the different painted finishes. Just choose the colors that you want from a color chart at the paint store, and the salesperson will mix it for you on the spot. It's worry-free.

Most paint companies offer large paint chips, about two inches by four inches, where their paints are sold. Collect as many as catch your eye—they're usually free—from all the different paint manufacturers, and mix and match them until you get the combination that appeals to you, and fits in with your home, your lifestyle, and your furnishings.

SIMPLE SOLUTIONS

The simplest and safest way to choose a color is to match it up to an existing fabric, carpet, or rug. If you are starting with a clean slate, pick the fabric for your couch or curtains first. With the infinite paint colors available, you can always find a match; it's much more difficult to work in the reverse, and a mistake with fabric is costlier to correct.

Choose one of the colors from the pattern that you really like, then take a swatch

This hallway has been given new life with a painted diamond floor and apple green walls.

of the fabric to a paint or hardware store and find that color among the paint chip cards. Each card will display four to six shades of a particular color, ranging from light to dark; this is called a color family. If you select one or two shades from the same color family, you can't go wrong.

If you are unsure about the moldings and trim, paint them white; it will make a lovely frame for the room. And I always prefer a white ceiling, which adds a feeling of height and openness to any room.

SPECIALTY COLORS

Even with the enormous color variety of water-based paints available, for some paint finishes in this book you may have to seek out special colors. A few finshes, like faux tortoiseshell, are a reproduction of the real thing, and for the most successful results it's always best to use true earth colors, which are found in a type of paint called artist's acrylics. Artist's acrylics may be more expensive than latex paint, but because these special finishes are generally applied to small surfaces, they're still economical.

If you are interested in returning an older home to its historic decorating roots, or want to give a new home some real country charm, most paint manufacturers now carry a special line of vintage or historic colors. These natural earthy tones are also found in milk paint, an old type of paint sold in powder form that is becoming increasingly popular due to the authentic finish it produces and its environmentally safe ingredients.

I am always delighted at how pleasantly surprised people are when they have taken the plunge and added a bold color or special paint finish to their home. If you just trust your instincts and go with what you love, you'll be delighted, too!

WHAT YOU NEED TO KNOW

The world of paint is constantly changing and improving, which can create a great deal of confusion. Before you begin any paint finish, it's important to understand the materials you'll need, and the required preparation.

Preparing a surface for paint, whether it's walls, floors, or furniture, is critical to the life of your finish. You don't want that beautiful painted pattern on your floor to lift off, or the seams of wallpaper underneath the paint to show through an elegant ragged wall.

I always find it better to split up the preparation time and the painting time. If you get everything ready a few days before you plan to paint, then you can really enjoy yourself when you start.

1. oil-based glazing liquid; 2. oil paint; 3. latex paint; 4. primer; 5. universal tint; 6. spray paint; 7. metallic powder paint; 8. artist's oil color; 9. artist's acrylic color; 10. stencil crayon; 11. Japan paint; 12. fabric paint; 13. spill-proof stencil cream; 14 and 15. craft stencil paint; 16. latex glazing liquid; 17. milk paint; 18. metal primer; 19. paint color samples; 20. powdered yellow paint; 21. milk paint powder; 22. latex block painting glaze

Decorating with painted finishes is an extremely inexpensive way to add design and character to your home. Most effects don't take long to complete; everything in this book is no more than a weekend project, and you'll enjoy your finish for years. If you do the job properly, you'll ensure an almost professional look. If you follow my recipes and instructions, I know you'll be thrilled with the results!

All About Paints, Glazes, Varnishes, Brushes, and Tools

Paint is the most versatile decorating tool you can find. Painted finishes can be applied to virtually any surface: all types of walls, doors, moldings, and trims; over wood, cement, and even linoleum floors; and as a finish or decorative accent on furniture. It's readily available to all of us, usually as close as the neighborhood paint or hardware store, and it's inexpensive.

There are two basic types of paint, water-based (latex) and oil-based (alkyd). If you visit a local paint or hardware store, you will be amazed by how many variations of these paints there are on the market: interior and exterior paints, powders, creams and sprays, acrylics, stencil paints, and even milk paint. As more and more people are doing their own painting and decorating, the less-toxic and odor-free water-based paints have become a popular choice. Thanks to new technology, latex paint is now more durable and versatile than ever.

Finding just the right paint color used to be a time-consuming, frustrating task. No more! Today there is an incredible range of colors available in a variety of shades. Each paint brand has a slightly different palette of colors, so if you can't find what you want at one store, look at the color chips for another brand. There are heritage or rustic color lines, as well as vintage colors for milk paints. Dark colors are more difficult to produce and aren't as popular as lighter shades, so there isn't the vast range in red or dark blue that you will see in the pastel colors. There are virtually hundreds of shades of white and yellow. Starting a collection of paint color chips is a great way to introduce yourself to the endless variety that's available. Once you get confident with color, you may want to experiment with universal tints and artist's acrylics to create your own custom-blended colors.

Glazing liquid, or glaze coat, is an essential ingredient for decorative painting. When mixed with paint, it slows down the drying time and allows you to work and blend the paint. Traditionally, glazing mediums or extenders have been available only with an oil base, and thus could not be mixed with latex or acrylic water-based paints. Because professionals and amateurs alike prefer the environmentally friendly properties of latex and acrylics, now water-based glazes are available from most major paint manufacturers. This is quite a revolutionary step—it means that most paint finishes can be applied easily with nontoxic water-based paints, glazes, and varnishes.

For all the finishes in this book, I have used only water-based paints and glazes.

After years working with oil paints, oil glazes, and paint thinners, it's marvelous to be free of the strong fumes and messy cleanup.

PAINT PROS AND CONS

Primer Primer is the key to most paint finishes; it creates a bond between the surface you want to paint and the paint finish you are applying. The right primer creates a solid, nonporous surface for the base coat by sealing new drywall, new plaster, concrete, raw wood, and any repairs you have made with caulking or spackle. If you miss this step, your paint job will be uneven and unpredictable. Primer should never be used as a base coat; however, if you want to apply a dark base coat, your primer can be tinted to half the formula of the paint color. This will reduce the number of coats required to achieve the desired depth of color.

Primer is available in acrylic, alkyd, and latex varieties; each one has its specific uses. Latex primer must be used over new drywall, as an oil-based (alkyd) primer will make the drywall's surface bumpy. For new wood, use alkyd primer, as water-based primer will soak into the wood and raise the grain, making an uneven surface. Thanks to advances in manufacturing, it's possible now to buy high-adhesion primers specifically designed to cover metals, ceramics, laminates, and most other shiny surfaces. These primers are wonderful because they save you a lot of hard work; for example, you no longer need to remove all the old varnish from a table or chair before you repaint, if you use the proper primer. Check with a knowledgeable salesperson to make sure you are buying the right primer for your project.

Shellac Shellac is an excellent primer for plaster and raw wood. Apply with a foam brush to seal in the wood resins found throughout the wood but especially at the knots. The resins will bleed through your paint finish unless you seal them first. Shellac is alcohol-based and dries very quickly. It's toxic, so wear a mask and work in a well-ventilated area.

Latex Paint Latex paint is water-based, and contains vinyl or acrylic resins. The better the quality, the more acrylic the paint contains. Latex paint is tinted to your color choice at the paint or hardware store using a recipe of concentrated color pigments, called universal colorants, that are both water- and oil-soluble. The same tints are used to color both types of paint. It is generally sold by the quart or gallon.

PROS
Fairly odorless
Dilutes with water
Wash brushes and tools with soap and water
Dries quickly; you can prime and paint 2 coats in one day
Preferable for exterior painting as its elasticity is better so it can accommodate weather changes
Hundreds of colors to choose from
Readily available in paint and hardware stores
Inexpensive

CONS
Dries too fast for some decorative finishes unless a glazing liquid is added
Will not adhere to oil-based paint or shiny surface

Oil Paint (Alkyd) Due to its oil base, this paint is smooth and easy to apply and covers the surface well. It is tinted to your color choice at the store using a recipe of universal colorants. It is available in pints, quarts, and gallons.

PROS Excellent coverage
Has the delayed drying time necessary for some decorative finishes
Can be applied over water-based paint
Readily available in paint and hardware stores
CONS Strong odor
Dries slowly, each coat takes 24 hours
Dilutes with paint thinner, never water
Cleans up with paint thinner

Artist's Acrylic Paint Artist's acrylics are sold by the tube and have the consistency of toothpaste. For decorative painting they are more often used to tint the glazing liquid. They are best used for projects such as a faux tortoiseshell finish, where pure colors lend an air of authenticity to the effect.

PROS Full range of colors including burnt umber, raw sienna, cobalt blue, thalo green, and metallics
Dilutes with water
Dries to a hard, scrubbable surface
CONS Expensive
Not economical for large areas
Dries quickly unless added to water-based glazing liquid

Artist's Oil Paint Artist's oils are tubes of thick, creamy, concentrated color. Professional painters use these oils to mix their own colors by adding small amounts to an oil-based paint or glazing liquid. Unless you are familiar with the basics of color blending, this is a difficult way to get the color you want.

PROS You do your own mixing, and the color is pure
Authentic colors for faux marbles and tortoiseshell
CONS Some colors are extremely toxic
Can only mix with oil-based paint (alkyd) and oil-based glazing liquid
Expensive

Ceiling Paint Ceiling paint is a less-expensive, lower-quality paint that comes in latex or alkyd, with a matte or flat finish perfect for ceilings. But marks and fingerprints show up easily, so never use ceiling paint on walls. You cannot apply a paint finish over ceiling paint because the paint is extremely porous, and the paint finish will sink into the surface.

Spray Paint Acrylic and alkyd paints, metallic finishes, faux stone finishes, lacquers, and urethanes are now available in spray cans. When applied carefully, spraying gives a smooth finish, free of brushstrokes, and the fine mist allows you to build up color one thin layer at a time.

PROS Good coverage for difficult jobs such as wicker furniture
Saves time when working on large stencils
CONS Toxic—the paint mist becomes airborne; wear a mask, and keep animals and small children away
Messy—cover up areas you don't want painted

Powder Powders are used by professionals to color any type of paint, glaze, or varnish. The color is very concentrated, so you don't need much. I use powders only for mixing metallic colors like gold, silver, and bronze. They are beautiful mixed with either oil- or water-based glazing liquid.

PROS Inexpensive
Endless variety of colors
Can mix with any type of paint or
glazing liquid
CONS Toxic—you must wear a mask when
mixing
Difficult to get the color you want
without a thorough understanding
of the basics of color blending

Milk Paint Milk paint is a mixture of milk protein, calcium, limestone, clay, and color pigments extracted from berries, coal, and seeds; it is sold in powder form that is then mixed with water. In North America, milk paints were blended by settlers with the natural resources they had on hand, and used to add color to wood furniture. Colors are limited to an authentic historic palette of subdued greens, blues, reds, browns, grays, black, and white. Milk paint should be applied only to raw wood for best results; it is not recommended for exterior painting.

PROS Nontoxic
Binds to wood fibers, giving long life
to the finish
Adds opaque color
Gives an authentic historic effect to
reproduction furniture
Is available in pure vintage colors
CONS Limited availability through some
craft, paint, and hardware stores
Does not cover up marks or stains
Needs a topcoat of oil, wax, or
urethane for protection
Cannot be applied over other paint,
stain, or varnish

Stencil Paint You can use most kinds of paint for stenciling, including spray paint. The key to successful stenciling is to apply the color in a dry or near-dry state. This prevents paint from seeping under the stencil, and also allows you to pick up and move the stencil along the surface without smearing the work you have just completed. You can also layer colors and add shading immediately. Choose a quick-drying paint, or some of the creams or paint sticks made for this purpose. If you're stenciling with latex paint or liquid stencil paint, it's important to keep your stencil brush as dry as possible. This is easily done by dipping your brush into the paint and then swirling the brush on a paper towel to remove the excess paint.

The specialty paints listed below are all available in craft and stencil stores as well as many hardware stores.

Japan Paints These are a favorite with professional stencilers. They are oil-based but dry immediately, they're durable, and they can be applied with brush or sponge.

PROS Durable
Good choice of colors
Applies over all types of paint as
long as the surface is not
high-gloss
CONS Liquid, can leak under stencil if not
used correctly
Patience required to build color and
shading
Cleans up with paint thinner

Creams and Crayons These are oil-based, with a semisolid consistency that translates into no leakage under the stencil. They should be applied with a stencil brush. Creams and crayons dry to the touch immediately, so you may build up colors and shading right away, and easily remove the stencil and replace it when creating a border without smudging. They can take several days to cure or dry completely.

PROS Nontoxic
Spill-proof
Durable once cured
Can be applied to fabric
Can be applied over any type of paint
as long as it is not high-gloss
A little goes a long way
Good range of colors
CONS Cleans up with paint thinner
Take a few days to cure

Craft Stencil Paints Sold in craft stores, these are liquid, water-based paints that dry faster than latex paint. They are the most common paints used by stencilers.

PROS Use with stencil brush or sponge
Good selection of colors
Dries fast
CONS Paint can leak under stencil if not
used correctly
Not good for scrubbable areas
unless you varnish over it

Ceramic Paint Made for application onto ceramic tiles, pottery, and urns, ceramic paints are sold in small bottles at craft stores. Some tiles, once painted, must be heated in a potter's oven or kiln to cure the color, and the paint colors will change in the heating process. Other ceramic paints do not require heating, but are not safe to use on dishes that you eat or drink from, and do not stand up well if washed or scrubbed. Read the manufacturer's instructions carefully.

PROS Great decorative accent for ceramics,
and can be used for painting and
stenciling
Use stencil brush or sponge
CONS Fairly durable, but better for areas
away from moisture

Fabric Paint Decorative fabric paints come in a wide range of colors, including metallics and phosphorescent shades. Some are water-based, some oil-based. Read the manufacturer's instructions for the proper application procedure and washing instructions. Don't use water-based paint on a fabric that normally reacts poorly to water, such as silk.

PROS Ideal for stenciling and painting on
fabric
Comes in many colors
Washable (follow manufacturer's
instructions)
CONS Not removable once applied
May fade after many washings

GLAZES

Glazing liquid, or glaze coat, has two purposes. By adding a glazing liquid to paint, you slow down the drying time, so you can manipulate and blend the colored glaze into whatever design or finish you choose. When creating faux marble, a colored glaze applied to a tabletop will give you time to

The amounts required for making a tinted glaze can vary, depending on the requirements of the glaze. A good guide is half paint and half glazing liquid, plus enough thinner to give the consistency of syrup. If the surface is vertical (e.g., a wall), the glaze will need to be thicker than if you are working on a flat surface (e.g., a tabletop). If you add more glazing liquid, the mixture becomes more translucent; if you add more paint, the mixture becomes thicker and more opaque.

In the past, double-boiled linseed oil was most commonly used as a glazing medium, and it is still being used today. Although beautiful to work with, there are disadvantages with this particular oil. It takes a long time to dry, often several days, it yellows, and it cannot be mixed with water-based paint. Today's oil-based glazing liquid has the look and consistency of custard, whereas water-based glazing liquid looks like milk. But both dry completely clear, and when added to paint change the color of the paint very little. They are usually available in quart and gallon cans at hardware stores.

Commercial glazes were first made up with an oil base, and could be mixed only

create the background drifts and veining reminiscent of real marble. Glazing liquid mixed with paint also turns the color from opaque to translucent. When you apply a tinted or colored glaze (glaze that has been added to the paint color of your choice) over a base coat, the base color will show through this translucent layer. For example, yellow-tinted glaze ragged over a white base coat will give the surface several shades of yellow. Not all decorative paint finishes require a glaze; for example, finishes in which the paint is applied directly onto the surface, such as sponging and ragging on, need only latex paint and water. However, if the paint must be manipulated to create the effect, as is required in ragging off, marbling, and combing, you must use a glazing liquid.

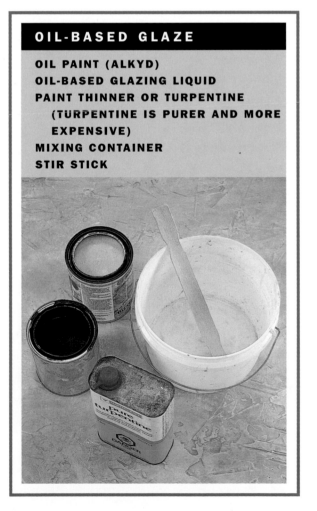

with oil paints. Now, because of the popularity of the more environmentally sensitive water-based paint products, water-based glazes are readily available. Most paint finishes can be achieved easily by using water-based paints and glazes. Keep in mind that different brands vary in their drying time; and it might be best to experiment and find the glaze that suits your needs before you begin a big project.

VARNISHES

There are many different types of varnish and many different names on the market, which can lead to some confusion. You may be more familiar with urethane, polyurethane, clear coat, or topcoat, but for clarity's sake I will use the term *varnish* throughout this book. Adding a coat of varnish has two distinct purposes. First, it protects the painted surface from bumps and scratches; second, it adds a sheen to the painted effect. Varnish, like paint, comes in several sheens from matte to high-gloss (see page 39 for descriptions of the sheens available).

Water-based and acrylic varnishes are suitable for finishes that have been created with water-based paint. They share the best qualities of any water-based product—they dry quickly and are odorless. But most important, they do not yellow as readily as oil-based varnishes, and their ability to dry clear makes all the difference to your painted finish, as yellowing will distort the colors and shades you have chosen so carefully. Water-based varnish cannot be used over oil-based painted finishes. Water-based varnish looks milky in

the can, but dries clear; oil-based varnish looks golden and will yellow with time.

Varnish on Walls There is usually no need to apply a protective coat of varnish to a painted wall. On a wall that has a decorative painted finish on it, the properties of the glaze used to create that finish offer adequate protection.

If the finish has been created with thinned-down latex paint instead of glaze, as would be the case with colorwashing, a protective coating should be applied, especially in a bathroom or kitchen. It's preferable to use a water-based varnish.

Application Before using, always stir the varnish well with a stick; do not shake the can or bubbles will form, which can cause a spotty finish on your surface. Use a sponge brush or low-pile roller to avoid leaving brush marks.

Varnish on Painted Furniture and Accessories Furniture, lamps, decorative accessories, or any items that are expected to withstand regular wear and tear require varnish for protection and sometimes for sheen. For example, a table with a faux marble top and ragged legs would need at least two coats of high-gloss varnish on the top, for protection and to give it the sheen of real marble. The ragged legs would need just one coat of varnish for protection and the sheen could be flat, semigloss, or high-gloss.

Application Working on small areas like furniture is relatively easy. There are special varnish brushes available, but I prefer disposable foam brushes, as they are easy to use, come in different sizes, are inexpensive, and do not leave brush marks.

Keep the area you're varnishing in as dust-free as possible. For a perfect finish, sand the surface with the finest sandpaper or steel wool between coats. If you wet down the area before sanding, you won't get scratch marks. This is known as wet and dry sanding. Make sure each coat of varnish is completely dry before sanding.

Varnish on Painted Floors As floors are a high-traffic area, all painted floors must be varnished with three to five coats for protection. Stained or painted floors look elegant and rich with a high-gloss varnish. For country-style painted floors, whitewashes, and stenciling, use a satin or semigloss varnish for protection. Water-based and acrylic varnishes are the best for finishes that have been painted with water-based paint: They dry quickly, are odorless, and do not yellow. Water-based varnishes cannot be used over oil-based painted finishes.

The topcoat you choose will determine the sheen on your floor: A flat sheen will disguise uneven textures or flaws better, a high sheen adds depth to your finish and highlights a smooth surface.

Application It is best to water down the first two coats of varnish, applying a very thin layer and building up from there.

Most varnishes were designed to go over wood, and yellowing wasn't an issue. But if you are applying varnish over light paint shade, yellowing will distort the color, so use a varnish that dries clear.

Note: Because of its size, achieving a smooth finish is not easy on a floor. You may save time and money by having a professional do this final step for you.

Sheens and Finishes

The sheen or gloss on your surface will come from your last coat, whether it's paint, glaze, or varnish. Paint manufacturers have their own names for different sheens, although most vary from matte or flat to pearl or velvet to semi- and high-gloss.

Note: The less sheen your finish offers, the less you will see imperfections; a high-sheen finish shows every drip, crack, and brushstroke.

MATTE

a flat finish

not very durable, marks easily

absorbs light, good for hiding imperfections

used mainly on ceilings

SEMIGLOSS

most commonly used for woodwork, trim, and furniture

reflects light, so surface marks or cracks are very visible

semigloss latex paint is an ideal base coat for painted finishes that require a great deal of manipulation such as faux marbles and tortoiseshell; it is easier to manipulate a glaze on a shiny surface

easy to wipe clean

EGGSHELL

also called satin, pearl, velvet

subtle sheen

very popular for walls as it's not too shiny, not too flat

ideal for mixing with glazing liquid

easy to wipe clean

HIGH-GLOSS

commonly used for exterior painting and doors because of its high durability

also used on interior doors, baseboards, and trim

reflects light, so any surface marks or cracks are very visible

adds depth to your finish

easy to wipe clean

Brushes and Tools

PROFESSIONAL

DRAGGING BRUSH Long-haired brush about 4″ or 5″ long. Very thick bristles, usually horsehair, that leave drag marks in the paint. (1A)

BADGER-HAIR SOFTENING BRUSH Made from badger's fur, extremely soft (the same bristles as used in men's shaving brushes). Very expensive, but ideal for softening or clouding the paint in finishes like faux marble. (2A)

STIPPLING BRUSH Square-shaped, flat-ended brush with medium coarse bristles. The handle is set at a right angle to the brush, and rotates. Used to stipple large surfaces. Comes in a variety of sizes from 3″ square to 8″ square. Expensive. (3A)

VARNISHING BRUSH Long-haired, natural bristle brush. Designed not to leave brushstrokes in the varnish. Expensive. (4A)

FITCH Natural bristles, long handle, comes in a variety of widths from ¼″ to 2″. Used for detail work and corners. (5A,B,C)

RUBBER COMB Triangular-shaped each side has different-sized teeth. Originally used for wood graining or faux bois. Commonly used for creating combed patterns. (6A)

METAL COMB Available in various sizes. Used for woodgraining or faux bois. (6B)

SEA SPONGE Large natural sponge with irregular holes that create a broken paint effect. Must be damp when used. (7A,B,C)

SWORD LINER Small brush, 4″ long, with soft bristles that are ½″ wide at the base and tapered to 1/16″ at the tip. Used for veins in faux marble. (8A)

STENCIL BRUSH Flat-ended brush used for stippling or swirling the paint onto a stencil. Available in a variety of sizes. (9A,B,C)

RAG Soft fabric used for creating an imprint in the glaze. Be sure to use only lint-free material. (10)

ARTIST'S BRUSH There are many sizes from 1″ down to just a few bristles for fine work. Price varies according to quality of bristles, sable being the most expensive. (11A,B,C)

ALTERNATIVE

long-hair bristle brush (1B)

soft bristle brush (2B)

wide bristle brush (3B)

sponge brush (4B)

standard 1″ paintbrush (5E)

homemade comb, cut from foam core (6C)

flat-edged hair comb

kitchen sponge made irregular by tearing bits off

feather, thin artist's brush (8B,8C)

kitchen sponge (9D)

old T-shirts make the best rags

any narrow paintbrush

BRUSHES AND TOOLS FOR THE DECORATIVE PAINTER

While there are many types of tools and brushes on the market, surprisingly, professional tools have changed very little over the years. If I had to invest in just one special brush, it would have to be a badger-hair softening brush. Even if you've never painted before, the effects you'll get from using this brush are just incredible. If you can, it's definitely preferable to invest in professional tools. They'll always make each job easier, and will give you the best finish. And if you clean and store them correctly, they will last you a lifetime. How-

ever, for every specialty tool, there is an alternative that can be found inexpensively in your neighborhood paint or hardware store, and I've listed it here alongside its professional counterpart. And often you can make some of the tools yourself. Sponge sticks, also called sponge brushes, are cheap alternatives to paint brushes and are especially good for varnishing. Throw them away after using.

Cleanup If you're going to invest in some of the marvelous brushes that are used for specialty finishes, or even ordinary paint-brushes, it's important that they are looked after so they will have a long life. After being used with oil or alkyd paint all brushes should be cleaned with mineral spirits (paint thinner), and when the paint is thoroughly removed they should be washed with warm water and soap. After being used with water-based or latex paint, all brushes should be cleaned with soap and warm water.

The professional brushes used for softening finishes such as faux marble get hard very quickly when you are working with a water-based paint or glazing liquid. If you feel the tips of the brush getting hard after about twenty minutes, rinse the brush under running water, shake it out, and carry on.

If you are not sure of the composition of the product you are working with, check the label or ask a salesperson what solvent is required to clean your brushes and other equipment.

Storage When the brushes are thoroughly cleaned and dried, they should be stored properly, either hung bristles down from a pegboard or laid flat and wrapped in newspaper or craft paper. This ensures that all the bristles will stay perfectly aligned and that the brushes will be ready for your next project.

Preparation

Preparation is critical to ensure professional results. If you skip steps or take shortcuts along the way to speed up the job, you will only be disappointed with the final results. For example, if you skipped the primer and applied latex paint over an old oil-based painted wall, your beautiful

Protect wooden moldings and trim with masking tape. Use low-tack tape over any painted surfaces. Cover floors and furnishings with drop cloths.

new finish could peel right off. No one likes the preparation stage, and you may be tempted to skip over parts, but in the long run you'll save time and money by being well prepared.

CREATING A SAFE WORK SPACE

• Take the time to create a safe working environment, giving yourself room to move freely. All furniture should be cleared out

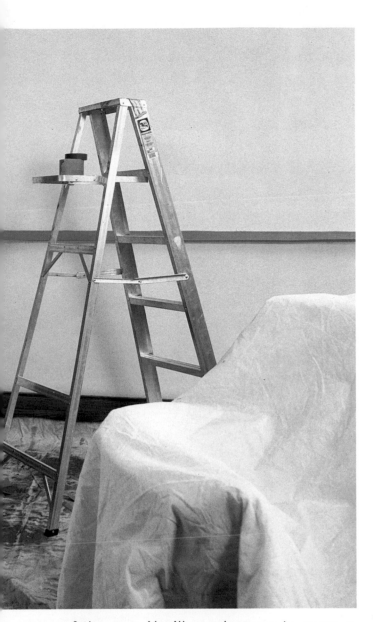

of the way. You'll need space to move a ladder around the room, and you won't have time to push the furniture aside as you go.

• Cover floors with painter's drop cloths. These are a good investment as they are reusable and paint won't seep through. Plastic on the floor is slippery and unsafe to walk on, and paint will seep through paper.

• Cover any furnishings left in the room with old sheets or plastic covers.

• Work in a well-ventilated area.

• Keep small children and animals at a safe distance.

• Whenever possible, work in natural light, or invest in painter's lights, available in most paint stores. Painter's lights are available as clip-ons or freestanding. They shed a uniform light so that you can see your progress when you are creating a decorative painted finish.

• Remove all electrical plates and hardware before you start. If your plates are plain white, lay them out on a sheet of newspaper and apply the same finish as the wall. They'll look much better blended in with your new finish.

• Always use low-tack painter's tape, available in hardware stores, when taping onto dry, freshly painted walls. Masking tape will pull off the base coat, and sometimes even the plaster.

• Wear gloves to save your hands. Medical latex gloves are the best, and can be bought in bulk.

• Have the tools, paints, and glazes close at hand, and review all instructions before you begin.

• When sanding, it's important to wear a dust mask and goggles to protect your eyes and lungs from airborne particles.

• When working with spray paint or powders, it is essential to wear a mask for protection from airborne toxic particles. For small jobs there are filtered masks that are effective for a short time (one day). For larger projects, or when working with toxic fumes such as those released by some paint strippers, there are more sophisticated masks with charcoal filters that you can change as they fill up.

PREPARING WALLS

Interior walls are composed of one or a combination of the following materials: smooth plaster, drywall, stucco, wood, veneer, or wood panels. You can paint over stucco to freshen it up, or intentionally give your stuccoed walls an aged appearance (see Painting Stucco, pages 87–89). Veneer paneling can be painted. But first, fix any holes or cracks as you would drywall. Paint will not stick or bond to dirt, grease, or a shiny surface. You will have to prepare any surface before you apply a paint finish. The aim is to roughen up the existing surface so the new paint can grab onto it.

Cleaning Remove loose dirt with a soft cloth or brush, or vacuum gently. Wash down greasy walls with TSP (trisodium phosphate), and rinse. Do not wash unpainted plaster or raw wood.

Repairs: peeling paint, cracks, and holes Scrap away any loose, peeling, or bubbled paint with a scraper, stopping where old paint is holding fast. For a perfectly smooth surface, you will have to add a thin coat of filler or caulking compound to the bare spots to eliminate the ridges where scraped surface meets old paint. Sand when dry, using medium sand paper. Finish off with fine grit paper. Brush away any loose paint and debris from holes and cracks. Moisten the edges slightly and fill with caulking compound. Apply two or three coats of caulking, allowing it to dry between coats, as it can shrink. Sand when dry with fine sandpaper. A good test to see if the surface is smooth is to apply a coat of primer over the patched area. If you can see where the patch is, sand down or add more filler. Prepare wood wall panels and wood trim the same way you do wood furniture (see pages 47–48).

Sanding It is important to sand any surface that has a high gloss before applying primer or paint. For an even finish, use a sanding block and work in a circular motion. Don't forget the trim and the woodwork. Sandpaper comes in different gauges. Your paint store salesperson will be able to show you which gauges suit your needs. After you have sanded, wipe down the walls with a damp mop or cloth. Allow to dry thoroughly.

Wallpaper To remove paper from walls,

Dark glaze was ragged over wallpaper to create this unusual textured effect.

wet down the paper with hot water until enough moisture soaks through to soften the glue, then scrape away the paper. There are solutions you can buy that will speed up the process, and you can also rent a steamer that will save time if you are tackling an entire room or removing many layers. Removing wallpaper is always a messy job, so put down canvas drop cloths to protect your floors from the water. Some papers will peel off dry, but leave a thin paper backing on the wall. This will peel as soon as you paint it, so it must be removed before you start. Dampen with a sponge and scrape off. After all the paper is off, wash down the walls thoroughly to remove any glue residue, and let dry.

It is possible to paint over wallpaper, as long as it is thick enough. Test first to ensure that the weight of the paint won't cause it to peel off. You will always see the seams, but if the wallpaper has a raised design, this will make an interesting pattern under a coat of paint. Ragging, color-washing, sponging, stenciling, or stamping are techniques that will add interesting texture and finishes over wallpaper.

Priming The primer coat is applied to seal the porous surface of new drywall, plaster, or wood, and the caulking or filler compound used for repairs. If you miss this step, you will get spotty coverage when you apply your base coat, as the paint will be absorbed unevenly. There are excellent primers on the market now that will adhere to almost any surface. Acrylic primer will cover old oil-based paint, shiny latex paint, vinyl wallpaper, and wood. You can paint over it within a couple of hours,

but it will take a few weeks to fully cure. Ask the salesperson for the correct primer for your surface. There is no need to prime if there is already a base coat and no repairs have been done.

PREPARING FLOORS

Painting or staining floors is often a scary prospect, as good preparation is needed, and decorated floors are often more permanent than painted walls. It's advisable to draw out a plan of the design on a roll of craft paper, whether it's a stenciled border, a diamond pattern, a faux tiled floor, or even a geometric design done with a stain. This will give you an idea of the effect and the proportions before you tackle the actual floor. Although painting floors is often more work than painting walls or furniture, they can dramatically transform a room for little cost. Paint adds life to badly marked or damaged wooden floors and disguises repairs that wood stains would intensify. The easiest floor surface to paint is wood; you can also paint concrete and subfloors, as well as linoleum, as long as the surface is properly prepared. It is not advisable to paint tile, ceramic, or unprepared linoleum floors as the paint will not adhere well. When the painted design is completed and dry, all floors should have between three and five coats of varnish for sheen and, most important, good protection.

Sanding Your first step when reviving an old wood floor will be to remove any wax, dirt, old paint, stain, and varnish from the planks. There are sanding machines you can rent that do a wonderful job and save wear and tear on your knees. But read the instructions carefully. Use a gentle touch or you will dent the wood. Generally, you will need to go over the surface twice, once with a heavy- and then with a light-grade sandpaper.

Sanding is a messy job. Remove all furniture and window treatments from the room. Keep cleanup to a minimum by closing off rooms you are not working on, and close the heating vents in the room where you are sanding. Always use a mask when sanding; the dust particles can be harmful.

Cleaning Allow the sanding dust to settle for a few hours, then sweep up dust and wipe the floor clean with a damp mop. Allow to dry thoroughly.

Repairs Use wood filler to fill in any large holes or cracks. Sand smooth with medium- or fine-grade sandpaper and wipe down.

Priming Apply an alkyd or acrylic primer to seal the wood. Water will soak into the wood from a latex primer and raise the wood grain.

Linoleum floors It is possible to paint over old linoleum floors, but you must prepare the surface properly. I recommend it as a quick-fix decorating solution that will only last for a few years, until you can afford to replace the floor. Thoroughly remove any wax, dirt, and grease from the linoleum using TSP, a heavy-duty cleanser available at your hardware store, rinse clean with warm water, then sand the surface to rough it up. When the floor is dry, apply a coat of high-adhesion primer, one intended for shiny surfaces. Let dry, and

proceed with your base coats and desired painted finish. Remember to protect your floor with two or three coats of varnish. As long as you follow the instructions you can paint any design you choose.

Cement floors You may paint over concrete, cement, or stone floors in basements or balconies provided you seal them first. Sweep up any loose dirt and dust, then apply one or two coats of acrylic primer over the dry surface.

FURNITURE

Finishing a piece of furniture with a fresh, new painted effect is a wonderful way to add personality to any room at very little cost. There are stores that sell ready-made unpainted furniture if you want to buy new pieces. Or build your own tables, shelves, and storage cabinets using the wealth of great ideas and materials in today's do-it-yourself marketplace.

Secondhand furniture can be easily found at yard sales, junk shops, and flea markets, or perhaps you have some pieces that you've inherited. These old finds are often well made, solid, and usually a bargain. It's also great fun scouring the streets and countryside for unusual finds. Here are some points to remember when looking for secondhand furniture to paint:

• The condition of the paint and varnish doesn't matter—they are easily removed.

• The color of the piece doesn't matter.

• Warped wood will always stay warped however well it's painted.

• Check all drawers and doors. If you are not capable of mending any broken draw-

This striking "rug" with a Navajo design was painted over an old white linoleum floor.

ers, legs, etc., don't bother with the piece.

• Small cracks are easily filled, but large cracks and holes are more difficult.

• Look for a piece that has an interesting shape and fits in well with your home's decor.

Preparing furniture for paint Taking the time to prepare your surfaces properly, be they odd tables, chairs, or other small accessories, will make all the difference to how long your finish will keep.

Stripping If layers of paint have been poorly applied, you will want to strip the piece down to its original surface. You can take the piece to a professional and have it chemically dipped. This saves time, but is not always possible, and chemical dipping will break down the furniture glue, so you may have a repair job on your hands.

There are stripping products on the market that you brush on. They dissolve the paint so that you can scrape it away. These commercial strippers can be hazardous, but there are some available that are less toxic. Always wear gloves, a suitable mask, and goggles to protect your eyes. Work in a well-ventilated area.

Another popular method is heat stripping. You can rent a heat gun for this purpose, but be careful not to damage the wood by burning the surface beneath the paint. Heat an area just until the paint begins to bubble, about 10 seconds, then scrape off the paint and direct the heat to another area of paint. After stripping, clean the wood with mineral spirits.

Repairs Repair any loose parts with wood glue. Fill holes and cracks with wood filler and sand smooth. Apply a coat of primer over the repairs. Any uneven spots will be more visible when the primer is on. Remove all hardware and clean it. You may want to buy new handles, as the old ones might not fit in with the new finish. There is a large selection of hardware on the market that will add greatly to your furniture facelift at little cost.

Sanding For tough jobs, start with medium-grade sandpaper and finish with fine or extrafine. Clean away the dust as you go with a tack cloth. Use steel wool for a final buffing. As much as possible, always sand in the direction of the wood grain; this helps to prevent scratch marks.

This yard sale find was transformed with a dragged effect and some freehand painting.

Don't press too hard or you will cause dents or gouges in the wood.

Primer Apply one or two coats of acrylic primer, sanding lightly with steel wool between coats.

Professional Tips for Painting Rooms

If you have never painted a room before, it may seem a bit daunting, but if you take it one step at a time and don't rush the job, you will be delighted with the results. For every project, follow these steps.

1. PREPARATION OF THE SURFACE

Paint will not adhere to dirt, grease, wax, or a shiny surface. Holes and cracks must be filled and sanded smooth, then the entire surface must be cleaned. Refer to Preparation, pages 44–45, for tips on how to prepare different types of surfaces. Repair and prepare the surface well, and the rest of the job will go smoothly and your finished effect will have a professional look.

2. PRIMING

When you have completed the preparation, you will need to apply a coat of primer if (a) you are painting onto raw wood, plaster, or drywall, or (b) if your surface is oil-based, and you are going to be working with water-based paints. You cannot put water-based paint over an oil-based paint—the paint will not adhere and will peel off when it's dry. Here's a tip on how to judge if your original base coat is oil-based or water-based: Apply a small patch of water-based paint to the wall in question and let it dry overnight; then, with your thumbnail, try to scratch off the paint. If it lifts off easily, your original base coat is oil, and you will need to apply a coat of primer.

Priming is an important step because it will ensure that you have a uniform surface over which to apply the base coat and painted finish. Refer to the Preparation section for the correct primer to use. If you haven't done so already, move furniture and carpets out of the room, and put down painter's drop cloths. Give yourself as much space to move around as possible.

Professional Tips for Painting Furniture

BEFORE YOU BUY
Secondhand furniture is a great way to furnish a home inexpensively. But make sure any damage is repairable. Paint won't cover up large gouges and cracks or replace a missing leg.

PREPARE BEFORE PAINTING
Refer to the section on preparing wood furniture (see pages 46–48) before you begin to paint. Note that high-adhesion primers are made to go over shiny surfaces, so there is no need to sand off all the old varnish or paint if it's in good condition.

CHAIRS
For best results, turn the chair upside down and paint the legs first, working toward the seat, and then paint the seat bottom. You can use either a bristle or sponge brush, but a bristle paintbrush will get into crevices and around spindles better. Once the legs are dry, turn the chair right side up and paint the back, then the seat last.

CHEST OF DRAWERS
Take out the drawers and paint them separately. Remove the handles, and fill in the holes if you are replacing the hardware. Either buy new handles or renew the old ones to enhance the new painted finish on the chest.

3. BASE COAT

This is step 1 in the instructions for most of the painted finishes. You will want to apply two coats of latex paint for best results. If the walls are white already, you may be tempted to skip the base coat and apply a finish such as colorwashing right over the old paint. But remember that you will be using a tinted glaze or diluted paint for the painted effect, and these are translucent, so any dark smudges or lines will show through.

Always work from the top down. By following this method you will avoid dripping onto finished work. Here is the order to follow when painting an entire room:

ceiling
walls
doors and trim
floor

4. PAINTED FINISH

Complete the base coats on the ceiling and walls first, then do your painted finish. If your doors and trim are to be plain paint, apply a fresh coat of paint to these areas when everything else is done. If you are applying a finish to the doors and trim, for example, faux marble or dragging, apply the base coat at the same time as the base coat for the walls. The last stage will be the painted effect on the door and trim.

The last surface to be painted or stained is the floor. If the floor needs to be sanded, do this after the walls are painted, as it's far easier to dust off the finished walls than to protect a newly sanded floor from ladder scrapes and paint drips.

Note: Be prepared to touch up the base-

boards after sanding, painting, or staining the floor.

5. PROTECTIVE TOPCOAT

You must apply varnish to walls only *(a)* when diluted water-based paint has been applied as a painted finish, for example, colorwashing or fresco, and *(b)* in high-traffic areas such as hallways, or in rooms with lots of moisture like bathrooms and kitchens. Unless you want a shiny surface, always apply a matte varnish which is invisible when dry. It's there only for protection. Floors always need three to five protective coats of varnish. And it is best to leave them for a week after you have finished the job before moving furniture back

This unusual faux finish door has been protected with two coats of varnish.

into the room, so they can dry thoroughly and harden. They will feel dry to the touch very quickly—within a few hours, but the first coat (varnish) takes several days to cure because varnish dries from the top-coat down.

PREPARE ✦ PRIME ✦ BASE COAT ✦ PAINTED FINISH ✦ TOP COAT

When painting, always work from the top down.

1. **Repair and sand all the surfaces: ceiling, walls, trim, and doors.**
2. **Prime all areas that have been repaired and any raw surface—wood or drywall.**
3. **Paint and finish ceilings first.**
4. **Paint base coats and painted effect on walls.**
5. **When walls are completely dry, paint trim and doors.**
6. **The last surface to be painted or stained is the floor.**

HOW TO APPLY PAINT

You will want to use a roller to cover large areas. But begin by "cutting in," painting a line next to trim and corners with a brush. If you find it difficult to paint a clean edge, then tape off the side you want to protect with a suitable tape (see below).

Don't overload your brush or roller with paint. It is easier to avoid drips and brush and roller marks when the paint is thinner. Although it's tempting to get the job over with quickly, your surface will be smoother and more perfect with two thin coats rather than one thick coat.

Working in sections of approximately 3 feet by 3 feet, apply paint in parallel bands using slightly crisscrossed strokes so that roller lines are eliminated. Work from the center of the section out so that the edges aren't repeatedly being loaded with fresh paint. Smooth out the paint from the center point toward the edges.

When rolling the ceiling, use a pole extender. You will be able to avoid drips falling on you, and it's easier to make long even strokes.

When rolling a floor, work from one side to the other, and move toward the door.

TAPE

There are different types of tape available for masking off selected areas you want to protect from paint.

Low-tack painter's tape will not pull off fresh paint when tape is being removed. You must use painter's tape when it is called for in any of the instructions in this book. It's reusable, which makes it economical when you are doing a large room, and will give you a professional finish.

Regular masking tape is much stickier than painter's tape, and is good for protecting the edges of floors or shiny woodwork or glass, where the low-tack painter's tape will not adhere.

TIPS: If you can't find low-tack tape, use masking tape but remove some of the stickiness by pressing a strip of tape onto a carpet or your clothing.

Smear some petroleum jelly around the edges of window glass or mirrors before you paint. Paint drips will wipe away easily, as the paint won't stick to a greasy surface. This step will save you from taping off each pane of glass.

FOUR MASTER TECHNIQUES

Although hundreds of effects can be produced with paint, most are created by using one or a combination of the four basic finishes that follow: color-washing, ragging, sponging, and dragging. Once you've mastered them, you will be able to produce any of the exciting effects in this book, from elegant faux marble, which is based on the ragging techniques, to aged plaster, which is based on colorwashing. If you're new to paint finishes, try these simple yet striking painted effects first. Start with colors that are similar in shade and tone for your base coat and glaze coat, so the effect will be subtle, and any mistakes invisible. Soon you'll see how easy it is to manipulate and work with paint, glazes, and different tools, and be ready for more challenging projects.

The walls in this inviting room have been painted with a simple colorwash of yellow ochre over a cream base coat.

Colorwashing

recipe

2 PARTS LATEX PAINT
1 PART WATER

Colorwashing is a distressed or broken-color technique that creates the illusion of faded plaster walls. It's most commonly used on imperfect walls to disguise cracks and bumps, but can also be used to add interest to smooth drywall surfaces. Colorwashing is one of the easiest and most effective wall finishes: Diluted paint is brushed on loosely, resulting in a variation of brush marks and a gradual buildup of color. The watered down paint is translucent, so each coat shows the one below. If one color is brushed randomly onto a base coat, a soft textured effect is created. Keep in mind that diluted paint is very runny, so this may be a messy job. Make sure the floors and furniture are well covered before you begin. And always work from the top down, or you will splash on the work you've just done. Colorwashed walls are perfect in any room, but walls in kitchens, bathrooms, and hallways should be given a coat of matte varnish for protection. Left, pale yellow and pink were applied over a white basecoat.

PAINT AND TOOLS

BASE COAT:
white latex paint, flat or satin
roller, brush, and paint tray

PAINTED FINISH:
latex paint, satin
1 mixing container
3" or 4" latex brush
paint tray

Step 3 Working in sections of about 3′ × 3′ or 4′ × 4′, apply the diluted paint in random crisscross brushstrokes, keeping a wet edge (see page 72). Continue to add the wash in crisscross strokes until there are no areas of the base coat showing. Let dry.

Step 4 If you're working in a bathroom, kitchen, or hallway, protect your colorwash with a coat of clear varnish.

TIPS: When you are painting on a large wall, keep a wet edge (page 72) so that you don't get join lines. When starting the next section, overlap your strokes by about 1″.

Always complete one wall before answering the phone or resting.

Colorwashing with Two Colors

If your first colorwash appears too bold, or if you want to add more texture to the finish, simply apply a second colorwash layer in a different color. Shown here: base coat white, first colorwash pale pink, second colorwash cranberry.

INSTRUCTIONS

For the best results, prepare your surface following the guidelines in the Preparation section (page 42).

Step 1 Base coat: Apply 2 coats and let dry for 2 to 4 hours.

Step 2 Dilute the paint for the colorwash paint with water in a mixing container as indicated, stir until mixed well, and pour into a paint tray.

ALTERNATE TECHNIQUE
Colorwashing with a Roller

For a large wall this is fun, and very fast. Use a short pile roller to apply the colorwash in criss-cross strokes. For a subtle effect the base coat

should be only a couple of shades lighter than the colorwashed coat. For a more contemporary and lighthearted look, try bright colors over white. Here I colorwashed the walls in emerald green, and I've added a burgundy border with freehand gold swirls and dots.

Ragging Off

recipe

2 PARTS LATEX PAINT
(THE SAME SHEEN
AS THE BASE COAT)
2 PARTS WATER-
BASED GLAZING
LIQUID
1 PART WATER

Ragging off is probably the most popular of all the painted finishes. A glazing liquid must be added to the paint when you're ragging off as the surface must stay wet long enough for you to manipulate the glaze with the rag. The most subtle effects are created by using soft lint-free rags—old T-shirts are my favorite. Chamois leather (used for waxing cars) gives the effect of suede, while crumpled plastic gives a more defined finish.

The key to successful ragging is the color combinations of the base coat and colored glaze. Soft colors over a white base will give the appearance of old walls. Dark colors over a lighter tone of the same color will create a dramatic, elegant effect. It's best to avoid mixing totally different colors, as these combinations usually look too sharp.

Use latex paint with either a satin or semigloss sheen; on the opposite pages, a dark forest green was ragged over a soft sage base coat.

PAINT AND TOOLS

BASE COAT:
latex paint, satin or semigloss
roller, brush, and paint tray
PAINTED FINISH:
latex paint, satin or semigloss
glazing liquid

mixing container
paint tray and medium-pile roller
2" brush
lots of rags torn into approximately
   12-inch-square pieces

INSTRUCTIONS

For the best results, prepare your surface following the guidelines in the Preparation section (page 42).

Step 1 Base coat: Apply 2 coats of latex paint and let dry for 2 to 4 hours.

Step 2 Mix the colored glaze as indicated and pour it into the paint tray.

Step 3 Apply the colored glaze: Start at the top of the wall and cut in the edges with glaze, using a brush. Next, apply the glaze with a roller to an area of about 3′ × 3′. Make sure 100% of the surface is covered.

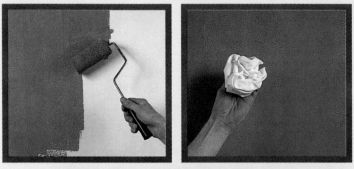

Step 4 Crumple up the rag so it looks like a rose.

Step 5 Dab the rag over the wet glaze surface. Keep turning the rag, and replace it with a dry one as it gets loaded with glaze. Do not overwork the ragging—dab about 70% of the surface.

Step 6 Move to the next section and apply more glaze with the roller. Overlap the wet edge of the previously ragged area. Rag off.

Step 7 Repeat the process of rolling on glaze and ragging it off until you reach the corner.

TIPS: Never stop halfway down a wall or in the middle, or you will get dark overlapping lines of color. If this does happen, redo the whole wall.

Always work from the top down.

Tape along the corners of alternate walls, and rag those walls first. When dry, transfer the tape and rag the other two.

ALTERNATIVES

You can vary the finish by ragging off the colored glaze with a variety of tools such as plastic bags, chamois cloths, and cheesecloths. Practice playing with the glaze to see which look you like. Below are some examples, but remember, everyone's touch is different. No two people will create exactly the same finish. That's part of the beauty of it.

Ragging with plastic (violet panel)
Ragging with chamois leather (dark green panel)
Ragging with cheesecloth (cherry panel)

Ragging On

**2 PARTS LATEX PAINT
1 PART WATER**

Ragging on is one of the simplest effects there is. It creates a less subtle effect than ragging off, but the advantage is that it can be applied without a glazing liquid. This is a textured effect that looks great on its own in children's rooms and makes a perfect background for stenciling. You can stencil right over the ragged wall or paint a band as a border around the room and decorate the border.

Ragging on ceilings is easy and does add to the overall appeal in this celestial bedroom. Just use a lighter touch than you would for the walls. When ragging, it's usually best to choose colors that are fairly close to each other, and the base color should be a few shades lighter than the ragged color. For example, rag yellow over a white base, or dark blue over a light blue. It's best to use the same sheen for the base coat and the paint you rag on.

PAINT AND TOOLS

BASE COAT:
latex paint, any sheen
brush, roller, and paint tray
PAINTED FINISH:
latex paint, same sheen as base

rags—cotton or T-shirt fabric is best
mixing container
paint tray
paper towels

INSTRUCTIONS

For the best results, prepare your surface following the guidelines in the Preparation section (page 42).

Step 1 Base coat: Apply 2 coats of latex paint and let dry for 2 to 3 hours.

Step 2 Dilute the paint according to the recipe and pour it into a paint tray.

Step 3 Crumple up the rag so it looks like a rose.

Step 4 Dip the rag into the paint and dab off the excess on paper towel.

Step 5 Apply the rag to the wall in random marks covering about 80% of the surface, keeping the pattern as uniform as possible.

TIP: If the effect looks uneven, apply a second coat in a different shade of the same color or in a second color.

ALTERNATIVE

Ragging on in 2 colors, for example, yellow over blue. Ragging on a second color adds even more texture to this finish, and can soften the overall look if you aren't satisfied with the appearance of the single color.

Ragging On

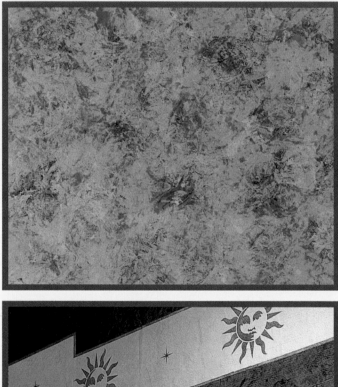

Sponging On

recipe

**2 PARTS LATEX PAINT
1 PART WATER**

Sponging on is the application of latex paint with a sponge directly onto the surface. It is fairly inexpensive because you are only covering about 80 percent of the surface with diluted latex paint. It's also a fast technique, as the paint dries quickly and the second coat can usually be applied as soon as you have finished the first, if you start in the same place.

It's important that the colors you choose contrast well, and I've found it is better to start with the lighter color as the base. The easiest method to make sure your colors complement each other is to pick two colors from the same family, such as a medium blue sponged over pale blue, or two colors that have the same depth or tone, like pastel yellow over a pastel blue base. Using the same sheen in the base coat as in the sponged colors will provide a more subtle effect. Using two different sheens will add depth.

PAINT AND TOOLS

BASE COAT:
latex paint, flat, satin, or semigloss
roller, brush, and paint tray
PAINTED FINISH:
latex paint, same sheen as base

1 container for each color to be sponged
sea sponges
disposable plates or paint trays
paper towels

INSTRUCTIONS

For the best results, prepare your surface following the guidelines in the Preparation section (page 42).

Step 1 Base coat: Apply 2 coats of latex paint and let dry for 2 to 4 hours. Don't forget, this coat will be one of the colors seen on the surface.

Step 2 Mix paint and water in the containers as indicated in the recipes. Pour each color onto a separate plate or tray. Wet the sea sponges so they are damp, not dripping.

Step 3 Start with first color. Dip one side of the sponge into the diluted paint and blot the excess on paper towels.

Step 4 Dab the sponge in an even pattern covering about 70% of the surface.

Step 5 When you have completed the first color and the surface is dry, use a clean sponge and repeat the process with the second color, and then third color as your pattern requires.

TIPS: Remember that the base coat will always be the least seen color, and the last sponged color will be the most dominant.

When you are working in the corners or along trim, break off a small piece of the sponge to avoid splotches or sponge marks.

ALTERNATIVE

The same three colors can give very different effects, depending on the order in which they are applied.

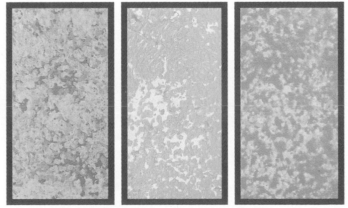

Sponging Off

recipe

**2 PARTS LATEX
PAINT
2 PARTS WATER-
BASED GLAZING
LIQUID
1 PART WATER**

Sponging off is a technique whereby a colored glaze is applied over a base color; the textured look is created by sponging over the wet surface. Sponging off gives a softer, more subtle effect than sponging on. As the drying time needs to be slowed down to sponge off, a glaze must be added to the paint.

PAINT AND TOOLS

BASE COAT:
latex paint, satin or semigloss
roller, brush, and paint tray
PAINTED FINISH:
latex paint, same sheen as base
    coat

water-based glazing liquid
mixing container
sea sponge
water
3″ brush
disposable plate or paint tray
paper towels

INSTRUCTIONS

For the best results, prepare your surface following the guidelines in the Preparation section (page 42).

Step 1 Base coat: Apply 2 coats of latex paint and let dry for 2 to 4 hours.

Step 2 Mix the colored glaze recipe in a container.

Step 3 Working on an area of about 3′ × 3′, apply the colored glaze over 100% of the surface. Always work in small sections to keep a wet edge.

Step 4 Dampen the sponge with water. Dab one side of the sponge over the glaze.

Step 5 Repeat step 3, overlapping the previously sponged area slightly, and dabbing off with the sponge. When the sponge becomes full of paint, rinse out with water.

Dragging

Dragging is the effect created when a dry brush is pulled through a colored glaze, revealing the base color in fine lines. When walls are dragged, they give the impression of silk fabric or a silk-look wallpaper. This effect is also called strié. It's a beautiful painted finish for a bedroom or living room, and is most effective in soft, pastel colors over a white base coat. An off white or cream base is ideal for vintage colors. You do need a fairly steady hand to drag the full height of the wall from ceiling to baseboard, but using a very wide brush, such as a wallpaper brush or even the end of a wide broom, will make the job faster and easier.

recipe

> 2 PARTS LATEX PAINT
> 2 PARTS WATER-BASED
>   GLAZING LIQUID
> 1 PART WATER

Dragging is most commonly used on doors, moldings, and trim. This will highlight the features and blends well with textured walls. Stencils work well over a dragged wall, and by painting a border around the top of the room in the base color and stenciling over the top of this border, a clean edge is produced.

Dragging is also an ideal finish for furniture, and works well with other finishes; for example, ragged walls look great with dragged baseboards. Use a semigloss paint, as you need a slippery surface for this technique.

PAINT AND TOOLS

BASE COAT:
latex paint, semigloss
paintbrush
PAINTED FINISH:
latex paint, satin
latex glazing liquid

mixing container
3″ brush
4″ dragging brush or any long-bristled
   paintbrush
rag
varnish (optional)

INSTRUCTIONS

For the best results, prepare your surface following the guidelines in the Preparation section (page 42).

Step 1 Base coat: Apply 2 coats of latex paint and let dry for 2 to 4 hours.

Step 2 Mix the colored glaze as indicated.

Step 3 Apply the colored glaze to a workable length of the surface. (For small areas like table-tops, cover the whole area.)

Step 4 Starting at one end, pull the dragging brush straight through the wet glaze. Repeat several times until you get the effect required.

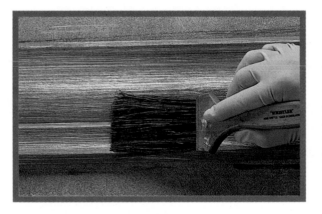

Step 5 Clean the dragging brush on the rag.

Step 6 Repeat on the next section of surface.

Step 7 Apply a coat of varnish for protection if the finish is on woodwork or trim.

TIPS: If you are working on a door frame, mask off the angle where the side and the top frames meet. Drag the adjoining area when the first dragged piece is dry.

Always drag in the direction of the grain.

Opposite, a cornflower blue glaze has been dragged over a white basecoat with a wide brush.

ALTERNATIVES

White base, yellow dragged (fresh look)
White base, vintage blue dragged (country or heritage look)

Finishes for

PART TWO

Walls and Floors

Although they've been around for hundreds of years, painted finishes applied to walls and floors are one of the fastest-growing trends in decorating today; their revival in the last fifteen years, first in Europe and now in North America, is quite remarkable. I'm often asked if this trend will wane, but in fact I believe today's newfound interest in decorative painting will remain strong. The cost of decorating surfaces with paper, fabrics, and stone is high, and although we may admire the rich look of silk or leather and the refined polish of marble, realistically these materials are not within many budgets. But with a bit of paint and a few inexpensive tools, all of these elegant looks are available to everyone.

Painted finishes are also ideal for camouflaging flawed surfaces or for adding new life and character to old walls and floors. For instance, by applying terracotta–tinted glazes to a wall that is marred or cracked, you can produce a textured look reminiscent of ancient frescoes; a simple colorwash will add instant warmth and appeal to plain white stucco.

Applying painted finishes to large surfaces using water-based glazes is faster and gives better results if two people work together. Usually one person applies the colored glaze while the other follows, removing or manipulating the glaze. To get clean, professional corners on walls, work one at a time, and mask along the corner of the adjoining wall with low-tack tape. This way you can work right into the corner without getting paint on the other wall.

The walls of this study have been softly colorwashed in two colors with yellow ochre over a cream base coat.

Leave the glazed wall to dry, then transfer the tape (low-tack tape is reusable) to the dry glazed wall and continue.

Always start by applying the glaze to the top of a wall and work your way down. Brush or roll the glaze onto an area of about 3 feet by 3 feet, then work the glaze to achieve the desired effect (ragging, flogging, etc.). Immediately apply the next section of glaze, overlapping about an inch along the edge just worked. This edge is known as the **wet edge;** if this edge dries, a seam forms in the paint, creating a line. This can spoil a painted effect, and is difficult to correct—if seam lines do appear, it's best to redo that wall.

A paint finish that looks truly professional never shows the tools used to create it. When your walls are completed, the impression should be of added texture or pattern, not of brush strokes or sponge blotches.

The floor is an important part of a room that is often overlooked when decorating— we tend either to put down wall-to-wall carpeting or to stain and varnish the wood in a plain honey or oak stain. But floors are important, and if your home has few interesting moldings or trim, why not make the floor a focal point? Many of the paint finishes described in this book can also be applied to floors. Character can be added to new wooden floors by colorwashing and then adding a decorative stencil; damaged old

An old linoleum floor has been transformed to look like a Mediterranean stone floor.

floors or unattractive imitation parquet can be easily disguised, and the look of tiles simulated—all with paint. Try painting a rug directly onto the floor (see Combing, page 107); it's a great idea for children's rooms or for a long hallway that needs a lift. Read the instructions (page 45) for preparing the floor before beginning.

Painted finishes are becoming more and more interesting and sophisticated as new techniques are discovered. Some of my most stunning paint finishes came about when I was correcting a mistake. If you're not happy with your results, for example, you've ragged a rich terra-cotta over a cream base, and the contrast is too great, try ragging over the terra-cotta with the base color. Everyone's touch varies, which makes each paint finish fresh and unique. It won't take you long to perfect these simple effects, and you will soon be inventing your own remarkable designs. Creating new looks is the best part of decorative painting.

CHAPTER 3

TEXTURED FINISHES

The interesting painted effects found in this chapter are all quick and easy to do, yet each one gives a distinctive look to any wall or floor. Frottage, bagging, and flogging add texture to a plain surface by the application and then partial removal of a tinted glaze. Each technique uses a different material—paper, plastic bags, or a long-bristled brush—to produce unique designs and textures when pressed into the glaze. With fresco and painted stucco, a tinted glaze is

applied randomly to the surface and then lightly rubbed off to imitate the appearance of worn, weathered walls. By colorwashing wood you have the advantage of adding color without hiding the natural wood grain. Plain wainscotting can be enlivened with a few coats of colorwash in interesting colors, and colorwashed floors make a perfect background for stenciling.

Yellow has been painted over a rough stucco wall to create a softly textured finish.

Frottage

r e c i p e

**2 PARTS SEMI-
GLOSS OR SATIN
LATEX PAINT
2 PARTS WATER-
BASED GLAZING
LIQUID
1 PART WATER**

The name frottage stems from the French verb *frotter,* meaning "to rub." This is a beautiful painted finish that is remarkably easy to do. Sheets of craft paper are pressed onto the glazed surface and gently rubbed, then removed—the technique is similar to bagging, but the results are more sophisticated. It looks best applied in rich dark colors over a lighter base coat. A frottaged finish has an elegant appearance that looks like soft suede—perfect for an entrance hall, dining room, or even bedroom. On the walls of this print room at right, ochre frottaged over pale yellow is accented with touches of faux tortoiseshell (page 154).

PAINT AND TOOLS

BASE COAT:
latex paint, semigloss
brush, roller, and paint tray
PAINTED FINISH:
latex paint, semigloss or satin,
   about 3 shades darker than the
   base coat
water-based glazing liquid

mixing container
3″ brush
paint tray and roller
a roll or sheets of craft paper cut
   into approximately 3′ x 5′-inch
   sheets
semigloss varnish (optional)

Frottage

INSTRUCTIONS

For the best results, prepare your surface following the guidelines in the preparation section (page 42).

Step 1 Base coat: Apply 2 coats of the base color and let dry for 2 to 4 hours.

Step 2 Mix the colored glaze as indicated in the recipe and pour it into the paint tray.

Step 3 Work in sections slightly smaller than the sheets of paper. Apply the colored glaze to the edges of the section with a brush and then fill in using a roller. The glaze should cover 100% of the work section.

Step 4 Immediately lay a sheet of craft paper over the wet glaze. Smooth it out with your hands.

Step 5 Remove the paper.

Step 6 Roll more colored glaze onto the next section, overlapping the glaze onto the edges of the previously glazed area. Don't stop working until you have finished a whole wall, keeping a wet edge the entire time (see page 72).

Step 7 To add to the depth of this paint effect, apply a coat of semigloss varnish when the paint is dry (optional).

TIP: Each sheet of craft paper can be used several times. Work with a friend, one person applying the glaze, the other working with the paper.

ALTERNATIVES

Frottaged painted finishes in green and red.

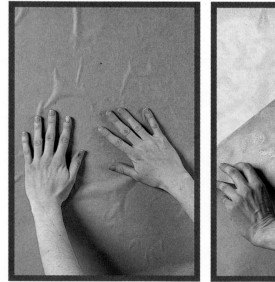

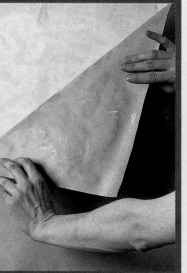

Bagging

r e c i p e

**2 PARTS LATEX PAINT
2 PARTS WATER-BASED
   GLAZING LIQUID
1 PART WATER**

Bagging is a technique that can produce many different effects, depending on the color combinations of the base color and the glaze color used. It's a simple process of rolling on glaze over a dry base coat and then laying on large plastic bags or sheets of plastic. By smoothing out the plastic that's stuck to the glaze, you create interesting lines and creases. By choosing specific colors and smoothing out the plastic in particular ways, you can create bagged finishes that look like leather and even marble. Here, the red glaze was bagged over a white base coat.

PAINT AND TOOLS

BASE COAT:
latex paint, satin
brush, roller, and paint tray
PAINTED FINISH:
latex paint, satin
water-based glazing liquid

mixing container
3″ brush
paint tray and roller
several garbage bags, sheets of
   plastic, or dry cleaning bags

Bagging

INSTRUCTIONS

For the best results, prepare your surface following the guidelines in the Preparation section (page 42).

Step 1 Base coat: Apply 2 coats of the base color and let dry for 2 to 4 hours.

Step 2 Mix the colored glaze as indicated.

Step 3 Cut the plastic bags down the sides to get very large sheets of plastic.

Step 4 Cut in the corners of the area to be painted with a brush, then apply the colored glaze with a roller. Cover an area about the same size as the sheet of plastic.

Step 5 Immediately place the plastic over the wet glaze and smooth the bag out. This forms the creases.

Step 6 Remove the bag.

Step 7 Repeat over the rest of the surface overlapping the glaze slightly to maintain consistency.

Finish one wall before stopping or you will create dark lines along the wet edge.

TIP: Bagging is a very fast technique—a whole room can be completed in a morning—but it is much easier to work with a friend, one person applying the glaze, the other bagging.

ALTERNATIVES

To create the look of leather, use rich deep colors such as dark red, tan, or brown over a base coat that's a couple of shades lighter. Smooth the plastic out so the creases run in different directions. Press in some upholstery tacks for an updated look that mimics leather, as in this border.

To reproduce simple faux marble, start with colors found in real marble, such as ochre, white, black, and green. Smooth out the plastic in one direction only, so the creases and lines run in drifts, emulating the veins of real marble.

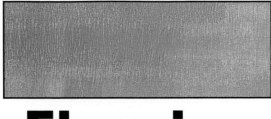

Flogging

r e c i p e

2 PARTS LATEX PAINT
3 PARTS WATER-BASED
   GLAZING LIQUID
1 PART WATER

The term *flogging* derives from the tool used to create this effect, a long-hair bristle brush known as a "flogger" that is similar to a dragging brush. A real flogger is expensive, but as a substitute you can use any 3" painter's brush with long bristles. Flogging is a technique that can be used in several different ways, from providing a background for faux wood to creating a silky textured effect on walls. A flogged finish is produced by applying a colored glaze to the wall and then flogging, or striking, the surface with the sides of the bristles. The base color should ideally be a few shades lighter than the glaze color, or you can apply the colored glaze over white or cream for a more distinct pattern.

Flogging on large surfaces with water-based paint and glaze takes practice, and you need to work fast. Always complete one wall before stopping, and always keep a wet edge or dark join lines will appear between the areas painted. Shown on the following page: soft green flogged over a white base coat.

PAINT AND TOOLS

BASE COAT:
latex paint, satin or semigloss
brush, roller, and paint tray
PAINTED FINISH:
latex paint, satin
water-based glazing liquid

4" brush
mixing container
flogging brush or any long-bristled
   brush
rag

INSTRUCTIONS

For the best results, prepare your surface following the guidelines in the Preparation section (page 42).

Step 1 Base coat: Apply 2 coats of the base color and let dry for 2 to 4 hours.

Step 2 Mix the colored glaze as indicated. Working an area of about 3′ × 3′ at a time, apply the colored glaze to the base coat in a crisscross brushstroke.

Step 3 Pull the brush vertically through the glaze to create a dragged effect.

Step 4 Hold the flogger so the bristles are parallel to the surface and then slap the brush against the glaze and lift up. Keep repeating this over the wet glaze, keeping the brush straight. This breaks up the dragged strokes.

Step 5 Repeat by applying more glaze to the next section, overlapping the sections slightly. Let dry.

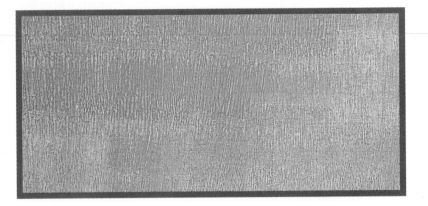

TIP: Keep the flogger as dry as possible by continually wiping any glaze off on a rag.

ALTERNATIVES

Pink glaze flogged over a white background.

Create an interesting pattern by flogging in two different directions, horizontal and vertical.

The walls in this city apartment were flogged in a soft green.

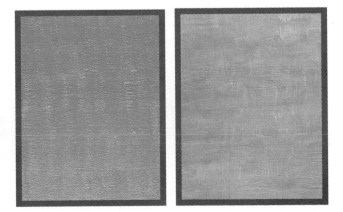

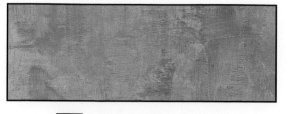

Fresco

recipes

For colored glazes:
2 PARTS LATEX PAINT
2 PARTS WATER-
   BASED GLAZING
   LIQUID
1 PART WATER
For whitewash:
2 PARTS WHITE LATEX
   PAINT
1 PART WATER

Fresco is the ancient art of painting on wet plaster using pigments and water, a technique which produces soft subtle colors that possess great depth. Although an ancient art, it's now one of the most popular finishes for walls and ceilings of both new and older homes. With the following recipe, this aged look can be achieved with the simple application of flat latex paint. If you choose warm Mediterranean colors, you can create an authentic frescoed wall like those seen in old Italian villas. Frescoed walls also make perfect backgrounds for stenciled or block-painted designs.

To create a frescoed finish first apply colored glazes randomly to the wall surface, blending them together slightly with a soft brush. After the glazes have dried, brush on a thin coat of diluted white paint. When some of this whitewash is rubbed away, revealing the colors underneath, the gentle look of a time- and weather-worn surface is created. In this living room, I've used two tones of pale gray, instead of the more traditional terra-cotta colors.

PAINT AND TOOLS

BASE COAT:
creamy white latex paint, satin
brush, roller, and paint tray
PAINTED FINISH:
pale orange/terra-cotta latex paint,
   satin
pale pink/terra-cotta latex paint,
   satin

water-based glazing liquid
creamy white latex paint, satin
3 mixing containers
several 3" brushes
paint tray
soft rags—pieces of T-shirt fabric
   are best, each approximately
   12-inches-square

INSTRUCTIONS

Fresco

For the best results, prepare your surface following the guidelines in the Preparation section (page 42).

Step 1 Base coat: Apply 2 coats of creamy white latex paint and let dry for 2 to 4 hours.

Step 2 Mix the glazes as indicated: First glaze coat is orange/terra-cotta; second glaze coat is pink/terra-cotta.

Step 3 With the 3″ brush apply the first colored glaze (orange/terra-cotta) to about 70% of the surface, with a brush using random strokes.

Step 4 Apply second colored glaze (pink/terra-cotta) to about 30% of the surface.

Step 5 Fold the rag smoothly so there are no creases, and dab onto wet surface to blend the colors and remove any visible brushstrokes.

Step 6 Pull a dry brush horizontally and vertically through the glaze to create random patterns. The look should be soft, with no brush marks. Let the walls dry completely.

Step 7 Whitewash coat: Dilute creamy white paint with water as indicated. Brush whitewash randomly over the surface.

Step 8 With rag folded smooth, dab out brush-strokes. Rub away some of the white paint to reveal more of the color underneath. Let dry.

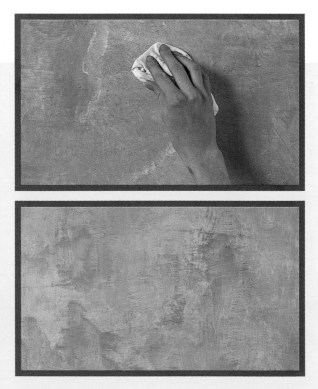

TIP: As the white paint dries, more of the base color will appear. For a more subtle effect, try a second coat of the white colorwash.

Painting Stucco

r e c i p e

2 PARTS LATEX
PAINT
1 PART WATER

I am often asked how to get rid of those pointy stucco ceilings that look like icing sugar and how to camouflage unsightly stucco on walls. Stucco removal is expensive; I find sanding down the points and plastering over the top with a smoother stucco to be a good, inexpensive solution.

Stucco on walls is now once again in vogue, but the new stucco has either a more polished, sophisticated look (often seen in restaurants) or is painted to highlight its texture; a soft colorwash of diluted paint works well. There are many brands of stucco on the market, each with different instructions. Ask your hardware dealer about the proper application. I like to apply the stucco with a thick-pile roller and then texture the surface with a wide spatula. If your walls are in bad condition, new stucco will hide the imperfections and provide a great surface on which to work.

A stenciled border combines beautifully with stuccoed walls.

Because stucco is plaster-based, it must be sealed before painting: Apply a coat of shellac with a short-pile roller.

PAINT AND TOOLS

PAINTED FINISH:
latex paint, low sheen
mixing container

4" brushes
rag

Painting Stucco

INSTRUCTIONS

Step 1 Seal the plaster stucco with a coat of shellac using a short-piled roller. Previously painted plaster should be given two coats of white latex paint.

Step 2 Dilute the paint with water as indicated.

Step 3 Working in an area of about 4′ × 4′ at a time, apply the diluted paint randomly over 70% of the stucco with a 4″ brush. Make sure the paint goes into the crevices.

Step 4 With a rag, blend and spread the paint over the stucco so that some of the paint is left in the crevices and some is brushed away. This will add an aged look, which is more fitting to a stuccoed wall.

ALTERNATIVES

Dull bronze for a contemporary look.
Fuchsia pink for a glamorous setting.

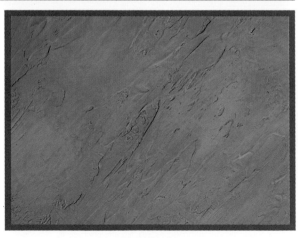

Colorwashing on Wood

r e c i p e

**1 PART LATEX
PAINT, FLAT
1 PART WATER**

Instead of applying coats of opaque latex paint, which hide the grain of wood, this technique of washing diluted paint onto stripped bare wood allows the natural patterns of the wood to show through. Staining floors with paint is an old technique, common in country cottages.

Colorwashing is similar to wood staining, but less expensive, and produces a more subtle, aged finish. There's also a huge range of paint colors available, as compared to a rather limited choice of colors for stains. Colorwashing is also effective on furniture and wainscoting, and makes a perfect base for stencils.

Make sure the wood is thoroughly clean of stain and old paint. If the wood has been stripped with chemicals, it must be washed down with vinegar and water, then left to dry completely.

The walls below were colorwashed first with blue paint, then with a second coat of green.

PAINT AND TOOLS

PAINTED FINISH:
latex paint, flat
4″ brush

lint-free rags
matte varnish

INSTRUCTIONS

For the best results, prepare your floor following the guidelines in the Preparing Floors section (page 45).

Step 1 If the wood is new, seal it with shellac to prevent resins in the wood and knotholes from seeping through your paint.

Step 2 Dilute the latex paint according to the recipe and brush onto the wood floorboards in the direction of the grain. Work on several boards at once, but try to cover the whole length of each board.

Step 3 Wipe the floor lightly with a rag folded so there are no creases, exposing the grain of the wood while the colorwash is still wet. The idea is to rub the paint into the wood, leaving a light coating so you can still see the grain. When the rag is full of paint, discard it and use a new dry one.

Step 4 Apply a second coat of colorwash if you want to build up the color, or to see less grain.

Step 5 Protect your new finish with 3 or 4 coats of varnish. A matte finish is preferable for colorwashed floors.

TIPS: Colors will look less intense when they are watered down and rubbed into the wood. The depth of color will vary with the number of applications.

Any stenciling should be applied when the paint is completely dry.

ALTERNATIVES

Three different colors:
- pale pink
- historic blue
- sea green

CHAPTER 4

PATTERNS

Creating patterns and designs on surfaces with paint is a great alternative to wallpaper or floor coverings. Paint is far cheaper, you can match up colors to furnishings more easily than you can with wallpaper, and you need just a roller and some primer to create an entirely new look when you want to change the design or colors of your room. Patterns can be applied to walls, floors, or even furniture in many different ways; for example, borders can be created with stencils, stamps, or household tools such as a comb, a kitchen sponge, or a bottle cork. Architectural features can be added, or existing features highlighted by combining a pattern such as a stripe, done below a chair rail, with a paint finish above. Any pattern applied to a floor, from diamonds to tartan, is a simple, inexpensive way to add character and charm.

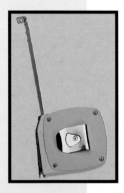

With a ruler and masking tape you can create crisp stripes and plaids; combs or sponges give a softer effect.

This simple staircase has been "countrified" with a yellow and green diamond dado and a faux rag rug runner.

Stripes

Stripes are a clever decorating tool and a quick solution to give the most ordinary room an extraordinary feel. Vertical stripes will make the walls look higher, while horizontal stripes make a room look more spacious. Although the preparation, marking, and taping take time, the actual painting of the stripes is accomplished quickly. Remember, the color you use as the base color will be one of the stripe colors. For example, if you're painting yellow stripes over a white base coat, you'll end up with yellow-and-white striped walls.

Although there are many ways to experiment with stripes, there are some basic rules that always apply. Walls should be smooth or your stripes won't be straight. The wider the stripe, the less taping and measuring there is to do. Here are a few tips on painting stripes.

Measuring and Marking the Stripes

• Stripes should be between 3 inches and 14 inches wide; any narrower and the walls will be too busy, any wider and the stripes will look heavy.

• If your room is a standard shape, measure all four walls and divide the approximate width of the desired stripe into this number until you get a width that fits evenly.

• Most rooms are not an exact size or shape so choose a width for your stripe and start measuring opposite from the least-seen corner. If you have a smaller stripe when you get back to that corner, it won't stand out.

• When you're working around windows and doors, just ignore them exactly as if you were hanging wallpaper.

• After deciding on the width of the stripes, mark around the top of the room with a pencil and a ruler or measuring tape. It's important to ensure your guidelines are perfectly straight. The professional (and easiest) way to do this is with a plumb line.

A plumb line is simple to make yourself. Take a length of light string the height of the wall, tie a weight to one end, and tie a knot in the other end; place a thumbtack in the knotted end. Stick the thumbtack into the first pencil mark at the top of the wall and the string will hang vertically. Pencil lightly along this line every foot until you reach the baseboard. You will always get a straight line this way. Repeat at each pencil mark. You can also use a chalked plumb line, following the same directions but omitting the pencil marks. Pull the string so it's taut, then

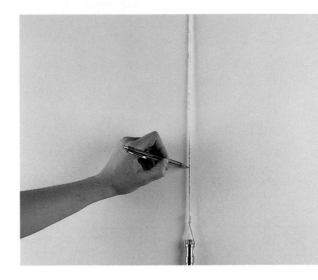

press it against the wall leaving a chalk residue on the surface. This can be easily wiped away later. When you've worked your way around the room, you're ready to tape.

Taping the Stripes Always use low-tack tape so you won't pull off the base coat when you remove the tape. Most low-tack tape is reusable, so you can tape half the room, paint, and then use the same tape again on the second half. Press the

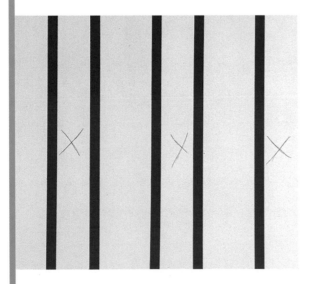

tape down along the pencil marks on the outside perimeters of each stripe to be painted. When you're finished taping, you will have the illusion of two different widths of stripes. The wider stripe is the one to be painted. To be safe, mark a light X in each "thin" section, the stripe *not* to be painted. It's easy to erase these marks. Don't mark the strips to be painted: You can't erase a pencil mark once the paint that is covering it is dry, and if you've used a light shade like the yellow we used here, it will show through.

Painting the Stripes The simplest method is to paint the stripes with a roller in a second color. Remove the tape immediately, and with a damp folded paper towel wipe away any paint that has seeped under the tape.

Alternatives There are dozens of alternatives for striped finishes. Here are two ideas:

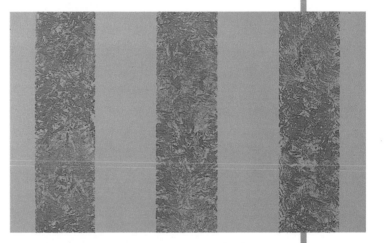

Ragged Stripes Follow the recipe for ragging on or off a wall, but apply it to the stripes only. Ragged stripes will create a rich, elegant look. Here the base coat is medium green and the alternate stripes have been ragged in a dark green.

Shadow striping: Vary the width and gloss of the stripes. Here the stripes are different widths, but the base color is flat latex paint and the stripe is high-gloss paint in the same color. A high-gloss varnish would achieve the same "shadow" effect. Using different sheens produces a bold, dramatic finish.

Squeegee Stripes

recipe

2 PARTS LATEX PAINT, SATIN OR SEMIGLOSS
2 PARTS WATER-BASED GLAZING LIQUID
1 PART WATER

Pulling a window-washing squeegee that has been cut with a pattern through a colored glaze creates fun and elegant stripes; this is one of my favorite finishes, and one of the easiest, as no taping or measuring is necessary. It's hard to get straight lines when you're applying this technique from ceiling to floor, but it's very easy from a chair rail down. Don't worry if the lines are not perfectly straight; this is a hand-painted finish, not wallpaper, and it should have character. Remember, as with all the stripe finishes, the base coat will be one of the stripe colors. At left we've added a console table painted to look like sheet metal.

PAINT AND TOOLS

BASE COAT:
latex paint, satin or semigloss
brush, roller, and tray
PAINTED FINISH:
latex paint, satin or semigloss—
  (the same sheen as the base
  coat); water-based glazing liquid
12" squeegee

craft knife
pencil and ruler
paper towel
3" brush
paint tray and roller
a second squeegee for filling in
  corners

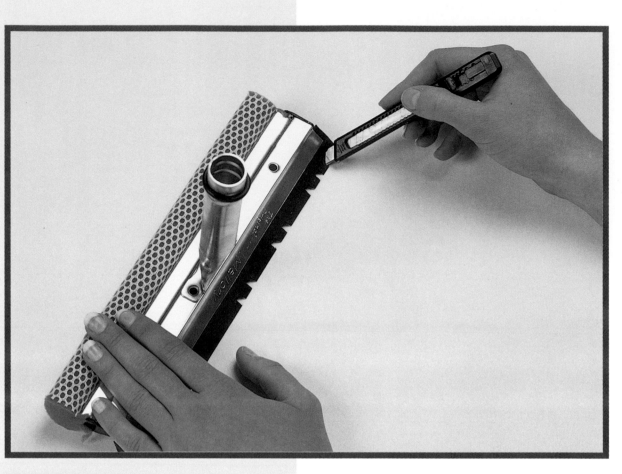

Squeegee Stripes

INSTRUCTIONS

For the best results, prepare your surface following the guidelines in the Preparation section (page 42).

Step 1 Base coat: Apply 2 coats and let dry for 2 to 4 hours.

Step 2 With a pencil and ruler, mark a pattern of teeth along the rubber edge of the squeegee. Keep the teeth ½" apart. Use a craft knife to cut out a wedge at every point.

Step 3 Mix the colored glaze as indicated and pour into the paint tray. First cut in with the brush around the chair rail and baseboard. Then apply an even coat to an area just over twice as wide as the squeegee.

Step 4 Starting at one corner and using a steady hand, place the squeegee at the top and pull through the glaze. Wipe the excess glaze off the squeegee. Then pull the squeegee through the next section.

Step 5 Repeat, overlapping the glaze slightly on the next section. Continue until there is less than a full squeegee length to the corner.

Step 6 Cut a second squeegee to the length that will just fit the remaining space up to the corner. Cut the same pattern into the squeegee, then apply glaze and pull the small section through. You may need to cut additional squeegee sections for the remaining corners.

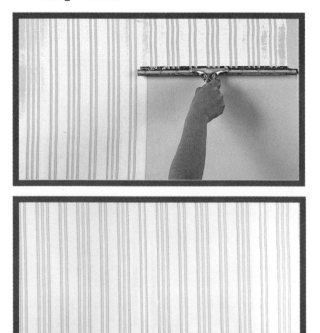

Stamping

Stamping is a fast and fun way to add patterns and designs to walls or furniture. The craft market has always had an enormous choice of rubber stamps, used primarily for personalizing notepaper, envelopes, and children's school projects. These stamps were traditionally rather small and the designs folksy. Now that home decorators are discovering this simple but effective art form, today larger rubber stamps with more sophisticated designs are available, such as roman numerals and even animal prints. The sim-

Stamped patterns and freehand painting enliven a plain armoire.

plest homemade stamp can be cut from a kitchen sponge, and, depending on the combination of colors and shapes you choose, you can create a variety of styles from country to elegant to bold ethnic motifs. The designs used for this technique gener-ally have straight edges and basic shapes—squares, diamonds, or stars are the most common—that are easy to cut out of a kitchen sponge with a utility or craft knife.

For more intricate designs, a new system has recently appeared on the market called block painting. Although it is a stamping technique, the results are more akin to stenciling, so I've included this technique in the Stenciling and Block Painting chapter (page 168).

Stamping Checks

recipe

**3 PARTS LATEX PAINT
1 PART WATER**

With stamping, you'll be surprised how quickly you can apply a border around the room, add accents to an old trunk or dresser, or create a checkerboard design. You'll never get perfect squares with the checkerboard technique featured here, but it's much faster than taping out all those squares. The look is rather fun, and can be as sophisticated as you want, depending on the colors you choose.

Here, the rich greens are quite elegant, but for a child's room you could use several colors in beautiful pastels, and red and white checks would make a perfect backsplash in a country kitchen.

The base coat should be latex paint in any finish except high-gloss. In the checkerboard design, the base color will be seen, so it should complement the stamped color.

PAINT AND TOOLS

BASE COAT:
pale green latex paint, matte, satin,
  or semigloss
brush, roller, and paint tray
PAINTED FINISH:
dark green latex paint, same sheen
  as base coat

kitchen sponge
craft knife
pencil and ruler
mixing container
disposable plates
paper towels

INSTRUCTIONS

For the best results, prepare your surface following the guidelines in the Preparation section (page 42).

Step 1 Base coat: Apply 2 coats of pale green and let dry for 2 to 4 hours.

Step 2 Make your sponge stamp: Cut the sponge in a square; 3″ × 3″ is a good size for a wall border stamp.

Step 3 Using the sponge square as a guide, mark along the top of the wall and up the sides every 3″ or the width of your stamp. This is a reference guide to keep the stamps straight.

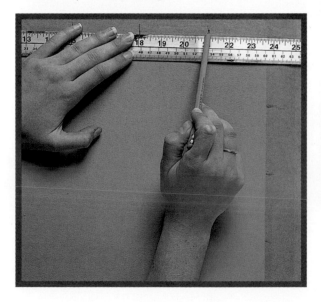

Step 4 Dilute the dark green paint with water as indicated and pour it onto a plate.

Step 5 Press the sponge into the paint. Then press the sponge onto a paper towel to remove the excess. Making sure the sponge is straight, press it onto the wall. Skip 3″ and then press on again. Work horizontally along each row, using the pencil marks along the top and down the side as a guide to keep the squares straight.

Rubber Stamping

There are many rubber stamp designs available in craft and art supply stores, but if you would like a design that is not available, you can photocopy the design and take it to a printing shop, where they will make a stamp for you. Here, colorwashed walls make a perfect background for stamping and gold paint.

PAINT AND TOOLS

BASE COAT:
latex paint, satin, *or skip* if you're applying over a completed painted finish like a colorwashed or ragged wall

PAINTED FINISH:
rubber stamps
ink pads *or* water-based paint
small roller and tray
pencil and ruler

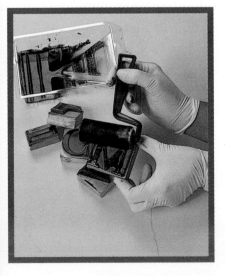

INSTRUCTIONS

Step 1 Base coat: Apply 2 coats of latex paint, if using, and let dry for 2 to 4 hours.

Step 2 Draw a guideline to mark where the stamps go. Use a light, erasable pencil. If you are stamping a border, pencil a straight line as a guide and pencil in a mark for the space between each stamp.

Step 3 Cover the design on the stamp completely with ink or paint: Apply the paint to the stamp with a small roller, rocking it back and forth, or press the stamp firmly into the ink pad and rock it.

Step 4 Press the stamp onto the wall surface, and again rock the stamp backward and forward to ensure you get a full impression.

Step 5 Remove the stamp carefully and repeat. Reapply paint each time you stamp to get an even look.

Step 6 Remove any pencil marks when all the paint is dry.

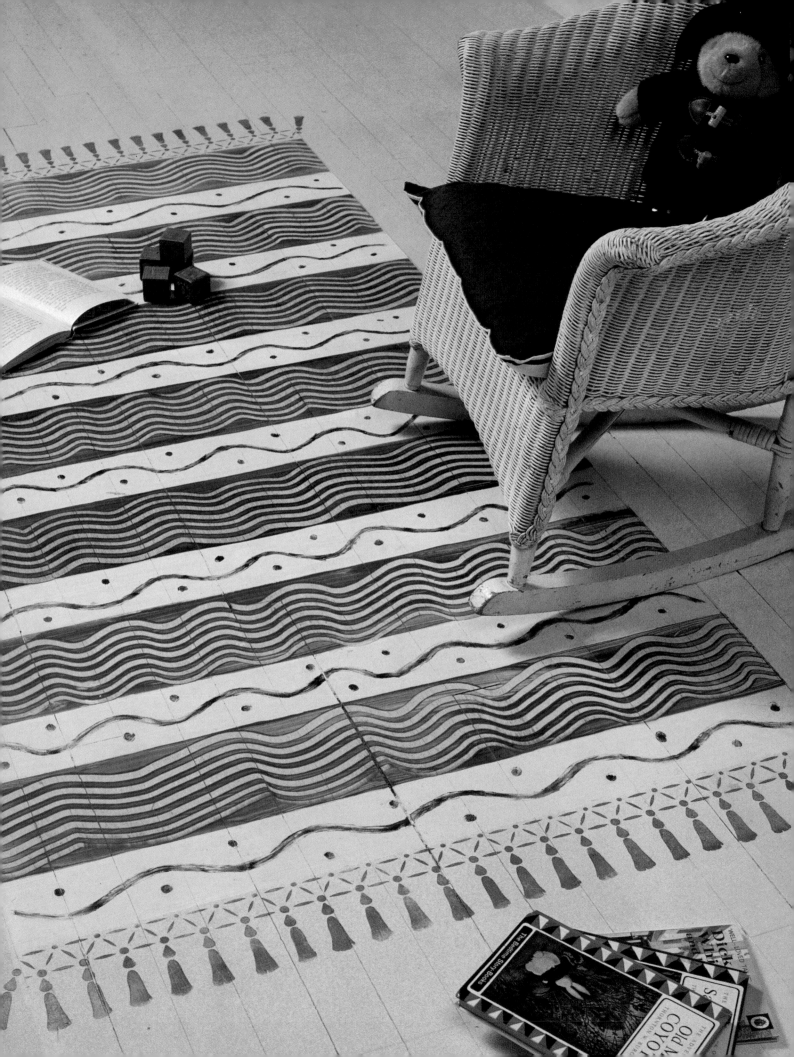

Combing

recipe

2 PARTS LATEX
PAINT, SATIN OR
SEMIGLOSS
2 PARTS WATER-
BASED GLAZING
LIQUID

A comb is often used by decorative painters to reproduce different wood grains, but it can also be used to create all types of designs and patterns on floors, walls, and especially furniture. There are several types of professional combs available in many different sizes, such as rubber triangles with different size teeth on each side, or even metal combs. The easier of these tools to use is the rubber comb, but homemade combs are both simple to make and easy to use. My favorite is cut from a piece of foam core, available in art supply or craft store.

Just cut a piece about 4 inches square, and at one end cut out even teeth ¼ inch wide and about 1 inch long.

A steady hand is required for combing. Avoid tackling the full height of a wall, as it is very difficult to comb straight lines while going up and down a ladder. Baseboards or furniture are really the ideal surfaces to work on. The most successful effects are produced by combing through a colored glaze over a white or pale base coat, but whatever color or pattern you do, a combed paint finish will always be stunning and unique.

PAINT AND TOOLS

BASE COAT:
white latex paint, semigloss
brush, roller, and paint tray
PAINTED FINISH:
blue latex paint, satin or semigloss
water-based glazing liquid
mixing container

low-tack painter's tape
pencil
rubber comb or handmade comb
small roller and paint tray or 3″
   sponge brush
rag

INSTRUCTIONS

Basketweave Pattern/Dado

For the best results, prepare your surface following the guidelines in the Preparation section (page 42).

Step 1 Base coat: Apply 2 coats of white semi-gloss paint and let dry for 2 to 4 hours.

Step 2 Put a length of low-tack tape along the top and down the side of the dado. Then, with a pencil, mark the width of the comb along the tape.

Step 3 Mix the glaze, and apply to a 4' × 4' section. Place a piece of tape to mark off this area.

Step 4 Pull the comb through the glaze horizontally until the whole glazed area has been combed in one direction.

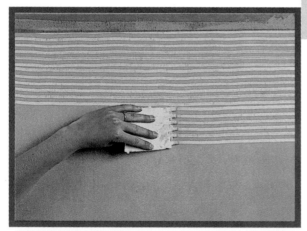

Step 5 Go back to the starting position and pull the comb vertically through the glaze to match the width of the comb, creating a square. Skip a space of equal size and repeat until the end of the row. Create a checkerboard pattern when combing subsequent rows.

Step 6 Apply glaze to another 4' section. Tape off. Repeat the horizontal and then vertical combing.

TIP: When you reach the corner, if the comb doesn't fit, cut out a small comb just for that space.

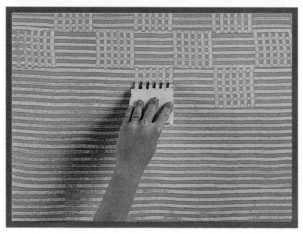

ALTERNATIVES

I found this dresser at a yard sale; it just needed some new hardware and a bit of paint. The combing design has transformed it into an elegant piece.

Vary your movements to produce a wavy pattern.

You can create a simple border using a home-made comb and a pencil eraser dipped in paint.

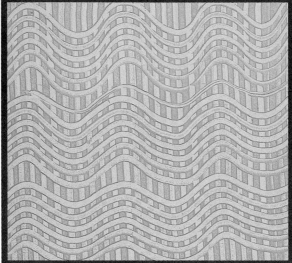

Terra-Cotta Tiles

Imitation tiles are a great paint treatment for imperfect wood floors. With staining or colorwashing, any repairs often remain visible and are not very attractive. Painted terra-cotta tiles cost a fraction of the real thing, and as a bonus they are not as hard and cold on the feet as stone and clay.

The technique is the same as you will find in the section on Stamping (page 101); there we use a kitchen sponge but in this case you cut a "tile" sponge out of a piece of upholstery foam. The most wonderful thing about this finish is that the tones for your tiles are mixed in such a way that you need stamp only once to get the effect. The grout lines will be the color of your base coat. It's not difficult—just a little hard on the knees—and the results are amazing.

Prepare the floor properly before beginning to paint, and finish off the job with three or four coats of mid-sheen or satin varnish for protection.

PAINT AND TOOLS

BASE COAT:
medium gray latex paint, satin
brush, roller, and paint tray
PAINTED FINISH:
terra-cotta and red/brown latex
    paints, satin
cream latex paint, satin
paint stirrer

paint tray and roller
4"-thick upholstery foam
craft knife
pencil and ruler
paper towels
2" brush
large aluminum tray or plastic sheet
semigloss varnish

Terra-Cotta Tiles

INSTRUCTIONS

For the best results, prepare your floor surface following the guidelines in the Preparing Floors section (page 45).

Step 1 Base coat: Apply 2 coats of gray (your grout color) and let dry 2 to 4 hours.

Step 2 Cut the upholstery foam into a square; 12″ is a good size for a floor. Slice off one corner. This will create a diamond pattern in the center of 4 tiles. Then cut a diamond shape to fit in that center. The diamond should be ¼ smaller on each of the sides than the diamond space left by the large square. This allows for the grouting space.

Step 3 Mark guidelines on the floor where the tiles will go, leaving a ½″ gap between each tile for the "grout."

Step 4 Pour some of the terra-cotta paint onto the

aluminum tray. Dribble a little of the red/brown over the terra-cotta. Swirl a paint stirrer through the paint, but do not overmix or the result will be muddy.

Step 5 Place the foam tile into the paint. Press down firmly to make sure the bottom is completely covered. Dab off any excess on a paper towel.

Step 6 Begin in a corner. Press the foam into place on the floor, then lift. Turn the foam 90° and press again. Repeat until you have 4 tiles with a diamond shape left unpainted in the center. Reapply paint to the foam every other square. Each tile should look different than the others. Repeat the pattern over the whole floor surface.

Step 7 If the foam square does not fit in awkward corners, cut a small piece of foam to size or fill in this area with a brush.

Step 8 Let the terra-cotta tiles dry. Then use the smaller diamond sponge to stamp in the centers with the cream paint.

Step 9 Apply 3 or 4 coats of semigloss varnish.

TIP: Test out the pattern and color on newspaper first

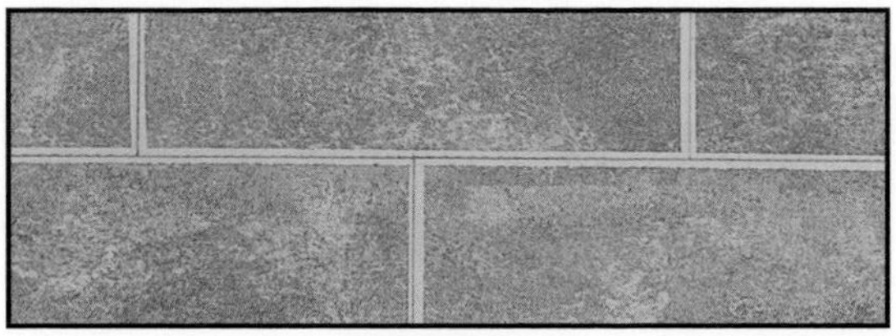

Stone Blocking

r e c i p e

2 PARTS LATEX PAINT
2 PARTS WATER-
   BASED GLAZING
   LIQUID
1 PART WATER

Stone blocking is a bold effect that will add instant character to any room. I usually recommend this finish for a hallway, entrance, or kitchen. Some people worry that the stone will be cold and impersonal. On the contrary, I think you'll find a stone-blocked wall painted in soft sand colors, beiges, or grays will be subtle and fresh in natural light and warm and inviting in the evening.

Although it looks like a complicated technique, it's actually very easy. It can be a lengthy process because of the marking and measuring of each "stone," but this really depends on the size of the room. It's important that the blocks of stone are the right scale for the room. A good size is 18 inches by 14 inches for a large room, and 16 inches by 12 inches for a small space like a vestibule. There

PAINT AND TOOLS

BASE COAT:
gray, cream, or white latex paint, satin
brush, roller, and paint tray
PAINTED FINISH:
latex paint in stone colors: sand, brown, gray, and white, satin sheen
water-based glazing liquid

mixing containers
disposable plates
sea sponges
pencil and long ruler or yardstick
cardboard
eraser
wide paintbrush—3" or 6" paintbrush
¼" low-tack tape

are several techniques for creating faux stonework, but the following is my favorite method; it's easy and a lot of fun.

The base coat will be the color of the groating or mortar; you can use gray, cream, terra-cotta, or white. If the walls are already coated with latex paint, just make sure that they are clean and there's no flaking paint. There's no need to fix any cracks, as they only enhance the effect. If you need to apply a new base coat, use one or two coats of latex in a satin finish.

Measuring, Marking, and Taping Stones

• Decide on the size of the stones. Make a cardboard template of one block and tape

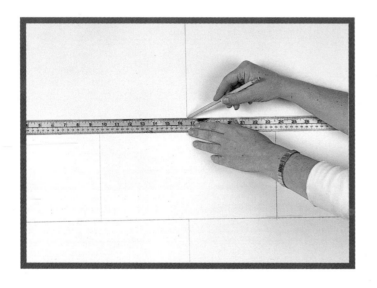

it to the wall to get a feeling of the scale you'll be working in.

• Starting in the top corner, mark along the wall with a pencil and ruler. To help you get the lines straight, use a level or T-square.

• A fast way to map out the stones in a small area is to cut a cardboard template and draw around this on the wall. Start in the top corner and work along the top row, keeping the board butted up under the ceiling or molding. For the second row, position the template halfway across the width of the stone above, imitating the placement of stones in a real stone wall.

• Using ¼-inch low-tack painter's tape, tape over the pencil marks. These will be your grout lines. After you have completed painting, and the paint is dry, erase the pencil marks.

• Add a coat of varnish for protection if working in a kitchen or bathroom.

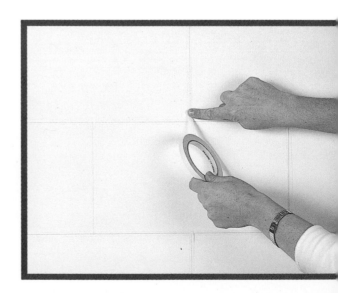

INSTRUCTIONS

Step 1 Base coat: Apply 2 coats of latex paint, either gray, white, or cream. Keep in mind that the color you choose will show through as the color of the grouting. Let dry for 2 to 4 hours.

Step 2 Mix your colored glazes as indicated. Because we're using water-based glaze, which dries

quickly, work an area of about 10 blocks of stone at a time. Apply the first colored glaze (sand) with a wide brush over 100% of the area.

Step 3 Pour the different stone-colored glazes onto paper plates. Make sure the stone colors are close in contrast; you can use 2 or 3 shades. Tear a damp sea sponge into small pieces.

Step 4 Sponge the second colored glaze (brown) randomly over each section of stone. Cover 80% of area.

Step 5 Apply third colored glaze (gray) to small areas. This is the natural markings of the stone; use sparingly.

Step 6 Repeat with white glaze (or any other colors you have chosen) sparingly. Make each stone slightly different. Realistically, one stone would

have more gray tones, the next more sand tones, and so on.

Step 7 While the colored glazes are still wet, go over the whole surface with a clean damp sponge, blending the colors together so they don't look too spotty.

Step 8 Remove the tape and when the paint is dry erase the pencil marks.

TIP: At the beginning, you may find 10 blocks too many to work on, as you must complete each step while the colored glaze is wet. You might want to start off working in a smaller area, but don't worry—you'll soon speed up.

Diamonds

This is one of my favorite painted floors. It looks particularly wonderful in hallways, but opens up and brightens any space. Although black and white diamonds are always stunning, other combinations work well also. For a more subdued effect, try pale gray and white; for elegance, try dark green and light green; and for a sunny children's room, pale yellow and blue make a cheerful play surface.

The actual painting of the floor is fast and easy, but the taping and measuring take time. Make sure the floor is prepared properly, and when dry, apply several coats of varnish so that your work lasts. It is difficult to achieve a smooth varnish finish on an area as large as a floor; I recommend hiring a professional so you're guaranteed a perfect finish. If the diamonds don't divide up neatly, you can always leave a border.

PAINT AND TOOLS

BASE COAT:
white latex paint, satin or semigloss
brush, roller, and paint tray

PAINTED FINISH:
black latex paint, satin or semigloss
pencil
measuring tape
chalk

low-tack masking tape
craft or utility knife
roller and paint tray
paintbrush
rag
varnish—the sheen depends on your
    taste, but high gloss looks great
    on black-and-white diamond floors

INSTRUCTIONS

For the best results, prepare your floor following the guidelines in the Preparing Floors section (page 45).

Step 1 Base coat: Apply 2 coats of white latex to the primed floor and let dry for 4 hours.

Step 2 Measuring and taping the diamonds:

(1) Measure the width and the length of the room and find the center point.

(2) Divide the width of the room by the proposed width of a single diamond. For example, if the room is 16' wide, the width of each diamond could be 2', which would create 8 whole diamonds across the width of the floor. If the length of the room is 17 feet, there would be 8 full diamonds and half a diamond at each end.

(3) Find the center of the room and measure outward. You want the partial diamonds at the sides, if there will be any, to be the same size. Make pencil marks on the base coat. When everything is marked, join up the marks with a chalk line, which may require two people.

(4) When all the diamonds are mapped out, tape the inside of each alternate diamond. Use a craft knife to cut tape corners cleanly. It's a good idea to mark the diamonds to be painted with a light cross so you won't make a mistake. The ones to be painted will appear larger.

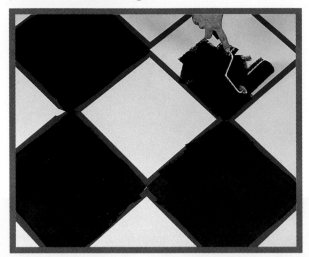

Step 3 Paint the black diamonds: With a roller and brush, apply 2 coats of the black latex paint to the marked diamonds. The pencil marks will not show through the black paint. Remove the tape and wipe away any seepage with a damp rag. Allow the floor to cure for 2 days.

Step 4 Apply 3 or 4 coats of varnish for sheen and protection. See Varnish on Painted Floors, page 39.

Diamond Dado

A diamond pattern looks fantastic on a wall, especially as a dado. Soft muted colors make a perfect finish for a country-style house, as on page 93. Rather than an opaque (solid) base coat, we brushed on a light yellow colorwash above and below the rail. The elongated diamond pattern was marked off with masking tape, and then, to create a more subtle effect, the colored diamonds were ragged and rubbed with a bit of green paint. The broken color in the colorwashed background and ragged diamonds adds irresistible charm to this design.

Tartan

Painting the look of tartan creates a whimsical finish that looks great in bright colors. Here, I livened up an old trunk with a base coat of bright yellow, and added black stitch marks and blue lines. This finish is appropriate for walls, furniture, and even floors. Flat surfaces are the easiest to work on; avoid carved surfaces, or ones with a busy design. The following recipe is based on a simple design, but if you want a more sophisticated pattern, you can copy a piece of real tartan fabric. The method will be the same.

PAINT AND TOOLS

BASE COAT:
bright yellow latex paint, semigloss
brush, roller, and paint tray
PAINTED FINISH:
black and blue latex paint

two ½″ artist's brushes
rag or paper towels
pencil and ruler
low-tack painter's tape
varnish—semigloss or high sheen

Tartan

INSTRUCTIONS

For best results, prepare your surface following the guidelines in the Preparation section (page 42).

Step 1 Base coat: Apply 2 coats of yellow latex and let dry for 2 to 4 hours.

Step 2 When the base coat is dry, mark off with a pencil where the pattern lines will go. Don't worry. The pencil marks will disappear under the opaque paint. Here, I've made a grid of 4″ squares.

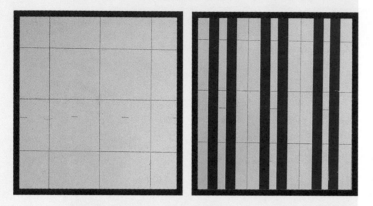

Step 3 Run 2 pieces of tape down the center of the squares in one direction, leaving a ½″ space between parallel taped strips.

Step 4 With a ½″ paintbrush and black paint, paint in each stitch mark using the tape as your guide. It may look time-consuming, but it goes very quickly.

Step 5 Remove tape. Repeat stitch marks running in the opposite direction.

Step 6 Paint over the pencil marks with an artist's brush and blue paint. These lines look best hand drawn, but if you want perfectly straight lines, retape for this step.

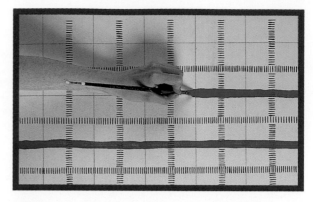

Step 7 Apply a coat of varnish for protection.

TIP: A little bit of glaze mixed into the paint makes it easier to make a straight line, but the paint will become translucent, producing a slightly different effect.

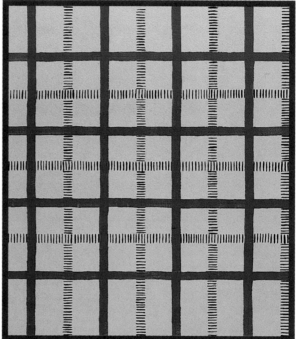

ALTERNATIVE
Plaid Floor

When you are painting any design on a floor, it's important to follow the guidelines in the Preparation section (page 45). I used historic colors that worked well with the milk paint on these kitchen cupboards. You can use milk paint on wooden floors, but the wood must be well sanded so that there is no residue of varnish or old paint (see Milk Paint, page 143). The actual painting for the tartan floor is very easy, but there's lots of measuring and taping. However, the results are well worth it!

For the tartan on this floor I used 4 colors of latex paint: cream, vintage green, gray, and burgundy. **Instructions:** Apply 2 coats of cream for

the base coat, and let dry overnight. Map out a grid of 2′ squares and tape alternate squares with low-tack tape. With a roller, paint alternate squares green. Remove the tape and leave the green to dry for a few hours. At this stage the floor will look like a green and cream checkerboard. Retape the cream squares on every alternate row, and roll gray paint over these taped squares. You will now have alternate rows of green and cream squares and green and gray squares. Leave to dry. Next, apply ½″ cream lines vertically and hor-

izontally down the center of the green and gray squares, and ½″ burgundy lines through the green and cream squares, vertically and horizontally. For perfect lines, run 2 strips of tape with a ½″ gap between the strips, roll on the paint line, remove the tape, and wipe away any leaks immediately with a damp cloth. Leave each line to dry for a few hours before taping off the next one. Let the paint cure for two days, apply at least 3 or 4 coats of low-sheen varnish for protection, and allow the finished floor to cure for one week.

CHAPTER 5

STONE FINISHES

From faux marble to granite looks, stone effects are the most interesting and most creative of all painted finishes. They are an art unto themselves, but one that anyone can master with a little practice. Once you've gotten your feet wet with the basic finishes like ragging and sponging, beautiful

faux marbles are just the next step.

Stone finishes add character to any room, whether in a rustic country cottage or an elegant town house, and they can be applied to a variety of surfaces—walls, baseboards, molding, trim, and, of course, floors and furniture. If you're not sure which colors to use or which stone you prefer, visit a tile store; collect pieces of marble and granite tile to see how the shapes and patterns are formed, and study stone walls to witness all the interesting shades and tones of real stone. If you're a beginner, it's best to start with small projects such as tabletops or fireplaces,

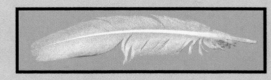

and then progress to trim and large areas, such as dadoes. Don't worry if you make a mistake—imperfections are often found in natural stones.

Clockwise from top left: Carrara Marble, Sienna Marble, Faux Granite, Easy Marble.

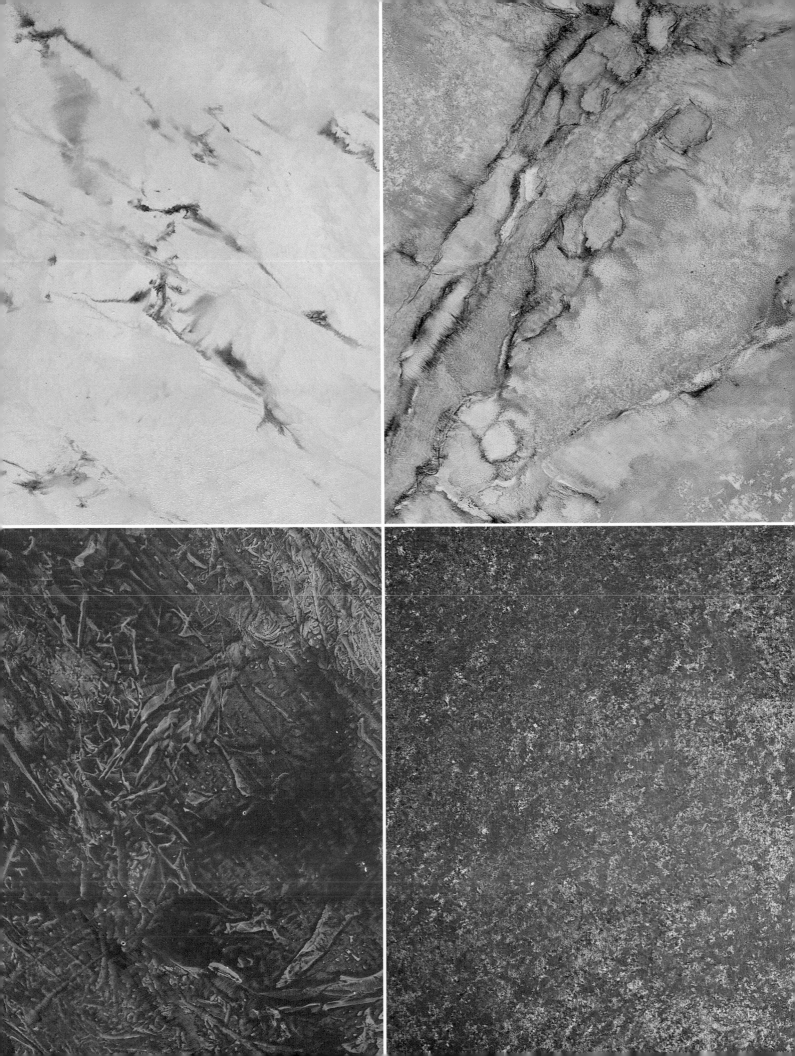

Easy Marble

r e c i p e

2 PARTS LATEX PAINT, ANY SHEEN
2 PARTS WATER-BASED GLAZING LIQUID
1 PART WATER

One of the most time-honored painted finishes, faux marble was traditionally applied to surfaces such as floors, tabletops, mantelpieces, and pillars, where the look of real marble was desired but unaffordable. Today, the look of faux marble is so popular that it can be seen on moldings, doors, panels, and fixtures where actual marble would rarely be used. Easy marble is a great effect for a beginner—you simply roll colored glaze onto the surface, then make a pattern in the glaze with a plastic bag, et voilà.

Realistically, marble would be installed in panels or sections. When applying a faux marble finish to your walls, divide the surface into panels. It is easier to work a small area, and your completed project will look more authentic.

When dry, a painted surface is more slippery when the sheen of the paint is high. So, use a base coat with a sheen, as the surface needs to be smooth and shiny in order to manipulate the colored glaze easily. The fireplace shown opposite features brown easy marble panels; the rest of the fireplace is faux granite.

PAINT AND TOOLS

BASE COAT:
cream white latex, semigloss
brush, roller, and paint tray
PAINTED FINISH:
red/brown latex paint, satin or semi-gloss

water-based glazing liquid
mixing container
roller
plastic garbage bags
high-gloss varnish

INSTRUCTIONS

For the best results, prepare your surface following the guidelines in the Preparation section (page 42).

Step 1 Base coat: Apply 2 coats of white latex paint and let dry for 2 to 4 hours.

Step 2 Mix the red/brown colored glaze. If you are applying the finish to a large space, work in sections of 3′ × 3′ or 4′ × 4′ at a time. Cover one section completely with glaze.

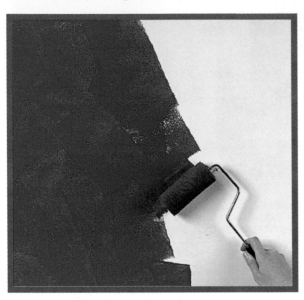

Step 3 Fold up the plastic bag like an accordian.

Step 4 Unfold the bag, place it over the whole surface, and smooth it out.

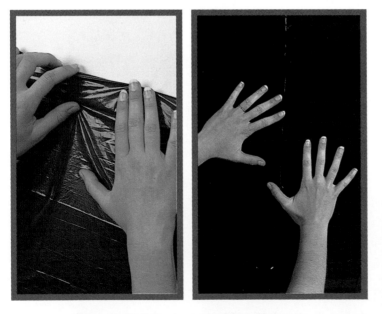

Step 5 Pull the bag carefully off the glaze, revealing lines and veins similar to those found in real marble. Move on to the next section.

Step 6 When dry apply high-gloss varnish for sheen and protection.

ALTERNATIVES

Here are two more examples of easy marble: green glaze over a white base and light sand glaze also over a white base.

Carrara Marble

recipes

For white glaze:
2 PARTS WHITE LATEX PAINT
2 PARTS WATER-BASED
 GLAZING LIQUID
1 PART WATER
For gray glaze:
2 PARTS WHITE LATEX PAINT
1 DROP BLACK ARTIST'S
ACRYLIC PAINT

Real Carrara marble comes from the town of Carrara in Italy, and is commonly used for floors, trim, and mantelpieces. The elegance of Carrara marble is easily reproduced with paint, and will transform a plain wooden fireplace or a tabletop into a stunning showpiece.

When reproducing the look of marble, bear in mind that real marble would be installed in pieces, so break your work up into panels, working one section at a time. You will want a smooth surface to work on, so it's important to sand carefully, and use a semigloss basecoat.

PAINT AND TOOLS

BASE COAT:
white latex paint, semigloss
brush, roller, and paint tray
PAINTED FINISH:
white and pale gray latex paint,
   semigloss
water-based glazing liquid
black artist's acrylic paint

mixing container
sponge sticks
soft rag—T-shirt fabric is best
feather or thin artist's brush
badger softening brush or soft-
   bristled paintbrush
high-gloss varnish

INSTRUCTIONS

For the best results, prepare your surface following the guidelines in the Preparation section (page 42).

Step 1 Base coat: Apply 2 coats of white latex paint and let dry for 2 to 4 hours.

Step 2 Mix the 2 glazes according to the given recipes.

Step 3 When the base coat is dry, use a sponge stick to cover the whole surface with the white glaze.

Step 4 Apply the gray glaze in drifts across the surface with a sponge stick.

Step 5 Rag the surface with a crumpled rag (see Ragging Off, page 59).

Step 6 Hold the badger softening brush at a right angle to the surface with a loose wrist and gently brush backward and forward, softening the glazes. The white and gray will become cloudy. Vary the effect by leaving some areas barely brushed.

Step 7 Mix equal parts black artist's acrylic and latex glazing liquid on a plate. Run the tip (about 1") of the feather through the black glaze.

Step 8 Holding the feather like a pen, gently paint veins running across the surface following the same direction as the drifts.

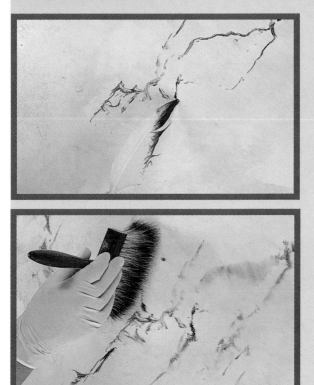

Step 9 Soften parts of the veins with the softening brush as described in step 6.

Step 10 Apply 2 coats of clear high-gloss varnish for protection and to emulate the sheen of real marble.

TIPS ON VEINING

Veining does take a little practice. Keep in mind that veins should be barely visible in places and stronger in other places; small veins should break off from the main veins periodically. Do not overvein.

Sienna Marble

recipe

**1 TABLESPOON
ARTIST'S ACRYLIC
RAW SIENNA
4 CUPS WATER-BASED
GLAZING LIQUID
2 TABLESPOONS WATER**

Sienna marble is an elegant marble that looks best on small areas such as moldings and trim, and in patterns on tabletops, lamp bases, and boxes. This is an intricate marble, so if you are not familiar with the way it actually looks, it might be best to visit a tile or marble store and take a look at the real thing. The technique for creating the look of Sienna marble is more complex than for the other marbles, combining black veins with irregular pebble shapes. Raw sienna artist's acrylic is essential for achieving a realistic result. Review Ragging Off (page 59) and Sponging Off (page 66) as you will be using these techniques to create this finish.

The base coat should be very smooth for a realistic marble finish. It's important to give the surface a good sanding before you begin.

PAINT AND TOOLS

BASE COAT:
creamy white latex paint, semigloss
brush, roller, and paint tray
PAINTED FINISH:
raw sienna latex paint *or* artist's
  acrylic paint
water-based glazing liquid
mixing container
black wax crayon

badger softening brush or a soft-
  bristled paintbrush
rag
sea sponge
3" brush
feather
water
turpentine
high-gloss varnish

INSTRUCTIONS

For the best results, prepare your surface following the guidelines in the Preparation section (page 42).

Step 1 Base coat: Apply 2 coats of off-white latex paint and let dry for 2 to 4 hours.

Step 2 Mix the glaze as indicated. Apply with a brush over 100% of the surface, if you are working on a small surface. If working on a large surface, like the wall below a chair rail, divide the wall up into panels and work on one panel at a time. If you are working on trim or molding, do lengths of about 4' at a time.

Step 3 With a bunched-up rag, dab over the wet glaze to break up brushstrokes.

Step 4 Hold the badger softening brush at a right angle to the surface and gently brush backward and forward to create a cloudy effect.

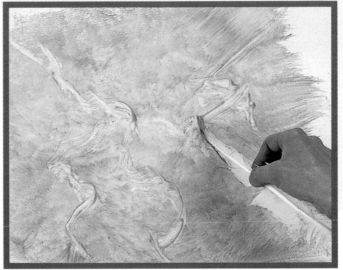

Step 5 Dip the feather in water, then pull the tip through the glaze in one direction. The water will open up the glaze, creating several veins.

Step 6 With a moist sea sponge, dab over areas of the glaze. Once again, the glaze should open up as it reacts to the water.

Sienna Marble

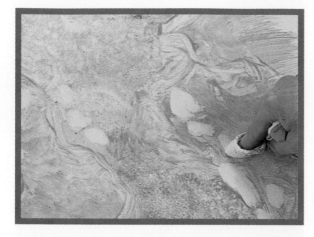

Step 7 With a rag wrapped around the end of a finger, wipe a few irregular pebble shapes along the veins.

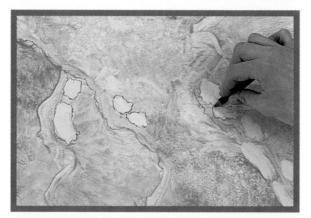

Step 8 Dip the end of a wax crayon into some turpentine to soften it. Draw a few veins following the pattern already created by the water. Draw around each pebble.

Step 9 With the rag, blot and soften the black veins so they blend into the marble.

Step 10 When the whole surface is dry, apply 2 coats of high-gloss varnish for protection and sheen.

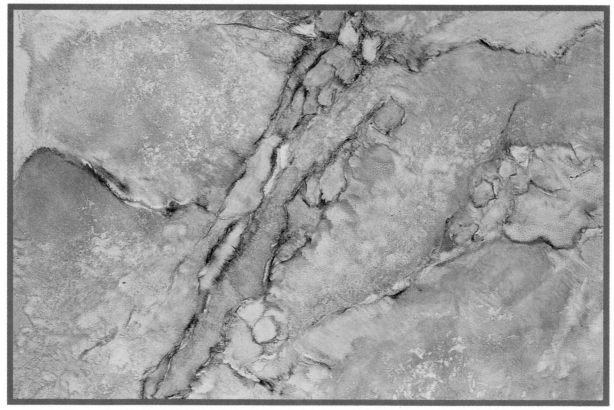

Faux Granite

r e c i p e

2 PARTS LATEX PAINT, SEMI-GLOSS
2 PARTS WATER-BASED GLAZING LIQUID
1 PART WATER

Granite is a hard, multi-flecked stone widely used on both interior and exterior surfaces. Its durability and rich handsome appearance have made granite a popular building material, but it is very heavy and very expensive. Simulating the look of granite is easy with the simple technique of sponging. The effect is created by applying layers of colors with a fine-holed sponge, or by using two sponges with different-sized holes. To look authentic, the surface must be very smooth, so sand it first thoroughly, and apply a high-gloss varnish not only to protect your work, but to give it the sheen and three-dimensional quality we associate with this stone.

Depending on the colors you choose, and the order in which you sponge them on, many different granite looks can be produced. Have fun creating your own design as we have on this tabletop, which features black, yellow, and white fantasy faux granite. I used a sea sponge with large holes, but to emulate real granite, use one with smaller holes.

PAINT AND TOOLS

BASE COAT:
latex paint, semigloss
brush, roller, and paint tray
PAINTED FINISH:
latex paint, semigloss, in 3 colors
water-based glazing liquid

mixing containers
sea sponges
plates or paint trays
paper towels
high-gloss varnish

Faux Granite

INSTRUCTIONS AND TIPS

• The same technique is used for creating faux granite as for sponging on, but slightly refined. The flecks should be smaller and tighter, and this can be achieved either by more layers of paint or by using a sea sponge with small holes.
• Colored glazes make the finish translucent.
• Let each layer dry before applying the next.

• When the surface is complete and dry, apply 2 coats of high-gloss varnish for protection and to give your work the shiny finish of real granite.

ALTERNATIVES

Here are recipes for 4 different but similar granites. Each features a different base color and three colors sponged on top.

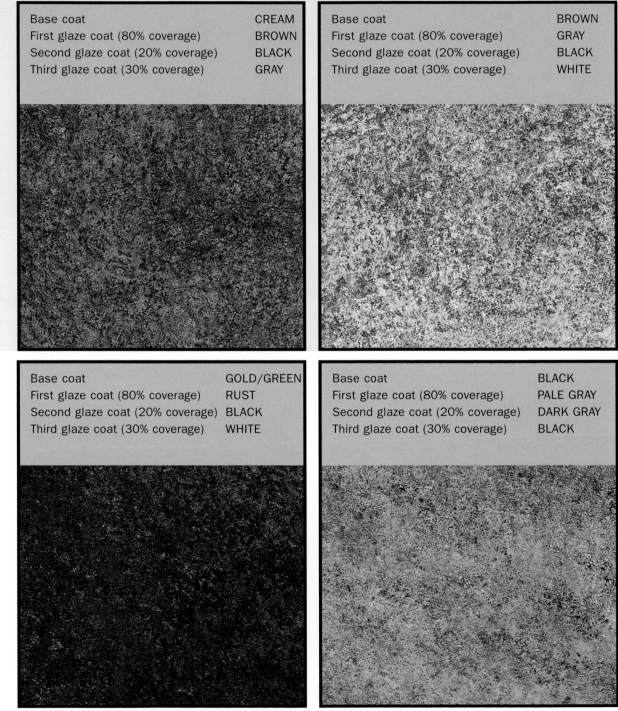

Base coat	CREAM
First glaze coat (80% coverage)	BROWN
Second glaze coat (20% coverage)	BLACK
Third glaze coat (30% coverage)	GRAY

Base coat	BROWN
First glaze coat (80% coverage)	GRAY
Second glaze coat (20% coverage)	BLACK
Third glaze coat (30% coverage)	WHITE

Base coat	GOLD/GREEN
First glaze coat (80% coverage)	RUST
Second glaze coat (20% coverage)	BLACK
Third glaze coat (30% coverage)	WHITE

Base coat	BLACK
First glaze coat (80% coverage)	PALE GRAY
Second glaze coat (20% coverage)	DARK GRAY
Third glaze coat (30% coverage)	BLACK

Finishes

for Furniture, Trim, and Accessories

We all have pieces of furniture that no longer look right in our homes, or pieces we've inherited or, in my case, furniture that came with a new husband! Often these furnishings are solid and well made—unlike a lot of today's pieces—but they look dated. As long as the shape is pleasing, it's remarkable how a piece can be transformed at little cost, quickly and easily, into a treasured heirloom. People often find tackling walls with painted finishes rather daunting, but feel more confident painting small surfaces. The projects then become fun, and are a great way to try out new ideas.

A fast-growing and favorite pastime is visiting garage and yard sales—it's amazing what I've found over the years. In fact, many decorative painters have started successful businesses by finding second-hand pieces, transforming them with painted effects and some new hardware, and then reselling them.

ANTIQUE AND SPECIALTY FINISHES

Aging new and reproduction pieces to have the warmth of well-loved hand-me-downs is easy and accessible with the glorious range of colors you'll find in the historic color palette. All you need is a bit of sanding to "wear off" the fresh paint in the places where these pieces would have been naturally worn over time. And there are now clever, time-saving techniques for producing crackled or weathered paint finishes, perfect for fixing up your own family heirlooms.

For small projects that will have a big impact on your room, nothing can surpass the glamour of a gilded finish or the exotic touch of faux tortoiseshell.

With the addition of a red crackle finish and some gold detail, a new mosaic-topped table takes on the look of an Eastern antique.

Milk Paint

Milk paint has been used for centuries to color and decorate household furniture and joinery; the recipe was brought from Europe to North America by the settlers. The basic ingredients, which include milk, lime, and natural colorants like berries, seeds, and minerals, were all found close at hand and inexpensively, and the result was highly durable paint whose quality is evidenced by the antique pieces we admire today that still boast their original coats of paint. Milk paint was not able to be mass-produced in liquid form because the milk protein caused the paint to sour, and in time the more convenient commercially produced oil- and water-based paints took over. Today, the unique beauty and durability of milk paint is once again available in powder form. It's popular as a finish for reproduction furniture, especially Shaker and Mennonite pieces, adds a period or country look to new interior kitchen or bathroom cabinets, and works well on a wide range of accessories from birdhouses and bread boxes to candlesticks and clocks. To make the paint at home, you mix the powder with water in a blender. You might wonder why you should go to the trouble of mixing, when

PAINT AND TOOLS

milk paint powder (see Resources, page 182, for purchasing information)
kitchen mixer (blender)
bowl
measuring cup
polyester paintbrush

0000 steel wool or 220-grit sandpaper
tack cloth or lint-free rag
wood sealer such as double boiled linseed oil, antique oil, antique paste wax, or beeswax

there are hundreds of premixed paints ready and waiting at any hardware store, but milk paint has special qualities that make it worth the extra effort for those interested in achieving an authentic historic finish. Unlike regular paint, which coats wood, milk paint actually sinks into the wood and binds to the fibers, creating a strong bond that will last for generations without chipping or peeling. It dries quickly to a hard finish that allows the natural grain of the wood to show through. Milk paint must be applied to raw or untreated wood or it will not be able to absorb and bind properly; if you put milk paint over regular paint or varnish it will peel off. Because it is absorbed by the wood, you will need to seal your finished project to protect it from humidity and spills. Use flat varnish or even beeswax for a truly authentic look. Instructions for historic finishing are included with most milk paint products.

If you want your newly painted heirloom

to have a more weathered look, rough it up with sandpaper or fine gauge steel wool by rubbing away paint in areas around handles and trim. There are instructions for

These milk painted cupboard doors were sanded lightly in areas that would naturally have become worn with age.

this aged or distressed effect under Antiquing (page 146). Omit the varnish undercoat when working with milk paint, and darken the new wood first with a non-sealing stain or a dark red milk paint wash so that the worn patches will have the authentic look of aged wood·

INSTRUCTIONS

Step 1 Mix paint according to the manufacturer's instructions. Remember that milk paint must be applied to new or previously untreated wood only.

Step 2 Apply paint evenly, overlapping the strokes as little as possible. Air bubbles will leave spots when they dry, so paint a few extra strokes to remove any bubbles.

Note: The surface will look chalky when it dries, but this will disappear when the sealer is applied.

Step 3 Lightly rub the surface with steel wool or sandpaper. This removes any milk paint residue, as well as any wood fibers that have been raised by the milk paint. Remove any dust with a tack cloth or lint-free rag.

Step 4 Apply a second coat for solid coverage. Sand lightly again.

Step 5 Use a suitable sealer to protect your project.

TIP: To check the color, paint a sample, let it dry for ½ hour, then rub on some oil. To produce a lighter color, add more water. For a darker color, apply 2 coats.

ALTERNATIVES

Milk paint can be used like regular paint for color-washing on new wood. It produces a translucent finish similar to a colored stain and enhances the natural grain and character of the wood.

You can also stencil with milk paint, but add less water to the powder because you will require a thicker paint for this decorating technique.

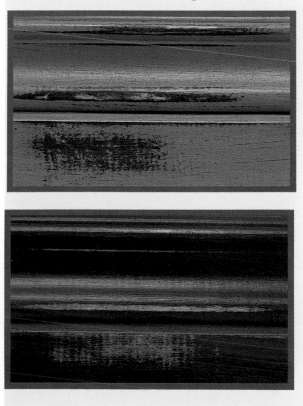

Antiquing

The idea of antiquing is to give furniture the appearance of old layers of paint that have weathered and worn over the years. Today's furniture is often made of cheap wood, and antiquing adds character to any piece. Paints that have a palette of rustic or heritage colors create the most authentic look of period furniture; these are muted colors such as off-white, brick reds, warm blues, and forest greens. Milk paint is available in all the original shades and also lends a genuine look to this finish.

Before applying water-based paint to new or stripped furniture, give the wood a coat of shellac; this will stop the paint from sinking into the wood and prevent any natural resins in the wood and knot-holes from bleeding into your paint. If you're working on painted furniture, apply a base coat before beginning your finishes. Choose an appropriate color as you'll see parts of it when the piece is sanded.

This sideboard was given a coat of shellac, then dark green paint, followed by a top coat of medium green, then sanded down to the wood.

PAINT AND TOOLS

BASE COAT:
white latex primer, satin
paintbrush
PAINTED FINISH:
at least 2 colors of latex paint, flat
　or satin sheen
paintbrushes
fine- and medium-grade sandpaper

steel wool
mixing containers and stir sticks
rags
varnish (optional)
toothbrush (optional)
oak stain (optional)
beeswax (optional)
matte varnish

INSTRUCTIONS

For the best results, prepare your surface following the guidelines in the Preparation section (page 42).

Step 1 Base coat: Apply 1 coat of latex primer.

Step 2 Apply a coat of light green to the whole surface, painting in the direction of the wood grain.

Step 6 The finished effect should show small areas of the base color, or the original wood, and a little more of the first color. The last-applied paint color will be dominant. For protection, add a coat of matte varnish.

TIPS: For an even more authentically aged look dip a toothbrush into dry stain, then rub your finger over the brush to flick small dots of stain over the painted surface, but be careful not to overdo it. As the paint dries, you can always wipe off the dots if the effect looks artificial.

As an alternative to varnish, put a little oak stain into some beeswax or furniture wax. Mix together well and rub over the whole piece. Buff with a soft cloth. This will give an authentic period look to the piece.

Step 3 When the paint is tacky or nearly dry, rub the "wear" areas with steel wool. The paint will come off easily. Remove more paint from places that would have had the most wear and tear on an actually old piece, e.g., around the handles, the edges, and over the trim.

Step 4 When the first coat is dry, apply the dark green paint to the whole surface. Paint over the areas rubbed down in step 3, always in the direction of the grain because some areas can be rubbed through each coat to the wood base.

Step 5 Let the dark green coat dry overnight and then sand off areas of paint with medium-grade sandpaper. Once again, remove more from around the handles, edges, and trim. Don't oversand. Keep stepping back to judge your work.

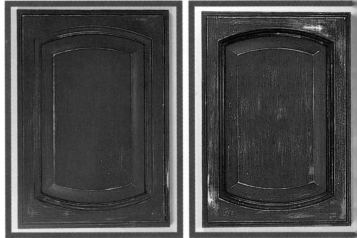

ALTERNATIVES

It's interesting to play around with different colors and combinations. Stick to the heritage colors for an authentic look. Above left, I used a light blue with a colonial blue as the top color.

On the right, I painted on first toffee brown and then dark brown over a cream base. To highlight the moldings I applied some brick red paint, and then sanded them back a little. Because they are recessed, they wouldn't be as worn as areas around handles and edges.

Crackle Finish

"Crackling" is one of the most popular finishes that I demonstrate on television or at home shows. A crackle finish simulates the look of paint that has aged and cracked. It's another wonderful way to enliven secondhand furniture and add character to new pieces. Although you can get varied effects by using different types of crackle varnish, I prefer a crackle medium that is available at craft and art supply stores and some paint stores.

The most exciting crackling results are from different combinations of color. Crackle medium is applied in between the base coat and the top coat. As the crackle medium dries, the base coat begins to crack. The top coat is then applied, and as it dries, it also reacts with the crackle medium and begins to crack and open up. The size of the cracks depends on the thickness of the layer of crackle medium— the thicker the coat, the larger the cracks; the thinner the coat, the smaller and more numerous the cracks.

PAINT AND TOOLS

BASE COAT:
latex paint, flat or satin—this
    will be the color of the cracks
PAINTED FINISH:
latex paint—flat or satin—this
    is the top coat, so choose the
color you want for the finished
project
crackle medium
2 paintbrushes
rollers and/or sponge sticks
varnish—low or high sheen

Crackle Finish

INSTRUCTIONS

For the best results, prepare your surface following the guidelines in the Preparation section (page 42).

Step 1 Base coat: Apply 1 coat of latex paint and let dry for 2 to 4 hours.

Step 2 Apply the crackle medium over 100% of the surface. If you want the cracks to be fairly uniform, apply the medium in an even layer. Varia-

tions in the thickness of the medium will produce different sizes of cracks.

Step 3 Let dry for about 2 hours. Different brands vary in the drying time, so be sure to read the instructions on your package carefully.

Step 4 Using even strokes, moving in one direction only, apply the top coat of paint over the crackle medium. The thicker the top coat, the thicker the cracks will be.

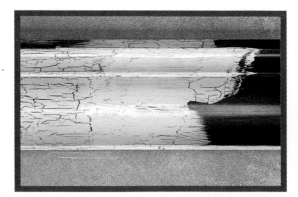

Step 5 Apply a coat of varnish for protection when the paint is completely dry. Low sheen gives an antiqued or aged effect; high sheen is good for a more contemporary effect.

TIPS: Practice first before tackling your project.

Drying the paint with a hairdryer will speed up the crackling.

The crackle medium and the paint can be applied with a roller or a sponge to produce different effects.

ALTERNATIVES

Remember, no two projects will ever look exactly the same. Everyone has a slightly different touch, and products vary, but this effect always looks stunning. Here are the color combinations for three different looks:

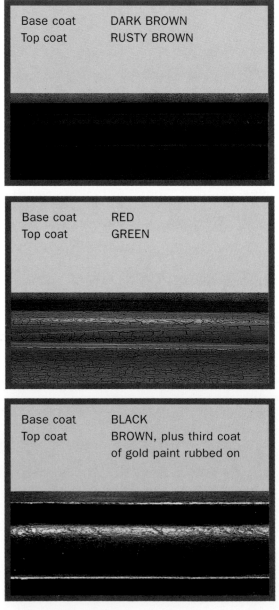

Base coat DARK BROWN
Top coat RUSTY BROWN

Base coat RED
Top coat GREEN

Base coat BLACK
Top coat BROWN, plus third coat of gold paint rubbed on

Aged Plaster

This easy finish is the perfect technique to give stark new plaster a more subdued look. Plaster sconces, pots, figurines, and moldings are readily available and inexpensive, but left as white plaster, they can look cheap and ordinary. By adding a touch of color and some whitewash you can highlight the cutwork and shape of your new piece, giving it the beauty and personality that comes with age. An aged plaster finish can also be applied to wood, plastic, or fiberglass, giving new trim the rich look of old-fashioned plaster moldings. Just make sure to prime the surface properly before you start painting, and use a white base coat.

PAINT AND TOOLS

BASE COAT:
(if required) white latex paint, flat or satin
paintbrush
PAINTED FINISH:
pale orange/terra-cotta latex paint, flat or satin

pale pink/terra-cotta latex paint, flat or satin
white latex paint, flat
water-based glazing liquid
paintbrush
soft rags
mixing containers

INSTRUCTIONS

For the best results, prepare your surface following the guidelines in the Preparation section (page 42). If you are working on new plaster, it must first be sealed, as plaster is very porous.

Step 1 Base coat: Apply a coat of white latex paint and let dry for 2 hours.

Step 2 Mix the orange/terra-cotta glaze and brush it on randomly, leaving spaces of white base coat.

Step 3 Mix the pink/terra-cotta glaze and brush it on over the spaces, overlapping the orange a bit. Let dry completely.

Step 4 Mix the whitewash. Brush it over the entire surface, making sure it gets into all the cracks and crevices.

Step 5 As the paint begins to dry—when it is tacky to the touch—polish the surface with a soft rag. This will leave the white predominantly in the crevices, creating the dusty look of old plaster.

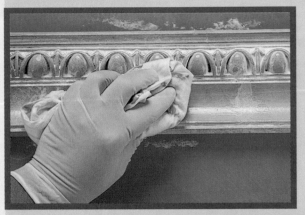

ALTERNATIVE

For a darker finish on this same angel sconce, I simply chose deeper shades of terra-cotta paint and rubbed away most of the whitewash glaze.

Faux Tortoiseshell

r e c i p e

2 TABLESPOONS
 ARTIST'S ACRYLIC
 PAINT
2 CUPS WATER-BASED
 GLAZING LIQUID
¼ CUP WATER

Because of its classic beauty, the look of tortoiseshell has been re-created by decorative painters for hundreds of years. The glowing browns, ochres, and umber of the natural seashell are reproduced by painting and softening using diagonal strokes. Faux tortoiseshell looks best on small, smooth surfaces; sconces, screens, door panels, and furniture are perfect for this sophisticated finish.

Here I have dressed up a plain wooden tray with a tortoiseshell panel; the red paint makes an elegant edging.

To reproduce a tortoiseshell effect, use artist's acrylics rather than latex paint, as the colors

will generate a more authentic finish.

PAINT AND TOOLS

BASE COAT:
pale yellow latex paint, semigloss
3″ sponge stick or small roller
PAINTED FINISH:
raw sienna and burnt umber artist's
   acrylic paints
water-based glazing liquid
black latex *or* artist's acrylic paint
two 2″ brushes

½″ brush
small artist's brush
sea sponge
low-tack painter's tape
badger softening brush or soft-bristle
   paintbrush
disposable plates
high-gloss varnish

INSTRUCTIONS

For the best results, prepare your surface following the guidelines in the Preparation section (page 42).

Step 1 Base coat: Using a sponge stick or roller to avoid brushstrokes, apply 2 coats of pale yellow paint. Let dry for 2 to 4 hours.

Step 2 Mask off the panel area with tape. Mix the raw sienna glaze and apply it in random diagonal strokes, covering the whole surface.

Step 3 Break up the glaze by dabbing the surface with a damp sea sponge.

Step 4 Mix the burnt umber glaze. With the ½" brush, apply it in irregular dabs working across the wet glaze and along the diagonal as in step 2.

Step 5 Draw black squiggles with the artist's brush in between the the burnt umber dabs.

Step 6 Holding the badger softening brush at a right angle to the surface, brush gently in a diagonal direction. The glazes should be softly blended. Do not overblend or the colors will become muddy. The last soft stroke should be on the diagonal.

Step 7 Remove the tape. I left a thin yellow outline (base coat) as a border around the tortoiseshell panel, and painted the rest of the tray red.

Step 8 Let dry and then apply 2 coats of high-gloss varnish for protection and sheen.

ALTERNATIVES

Red tortoiseshell over a pinky-red basecoat.

METALLIC FINISHES

From the ornate look of gilding to the weathered effects of verdigris and faux rust, surfaces that give the illusion of a metal finish have become extremely popular in recent years. Although metallic finishes are often used to decorate walls in offices, restaurants, in the home they're most suited to furniture, accessories, and trim. Exposed to the atmosphere, real metals such as bronze, copper, lead, and brass will naturally tarnish and corrode, acquiring a smooth patina. Happily, this lovely patination can easily be simulated with paint, not only on metal objects but on wood, pottery, and even plaster. New terracotta pots, wooden window boxes, and even lamp bases can be antiqued so that they look as though they were crafted years ago. Gold and silver finishes can make the most ordinary object luxurious. For a more contemporary effect, silver sheet metal is an interesting finish, ideal for flat surfaces like tabletops, screens, or even walls.

This homemade ladder has been given a faux rust treatment and now makes a great decorative (and practical) shelf unit.

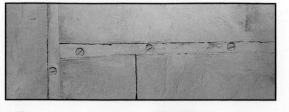

Sheet Metal

r e c i p e

**2 PARTS SILVER
LATEX PAINT
1 PART WATER-BASED
GLAZING LIQUID**
OR
**3 TABLESPOONS
SILVER POWDER
1 CUP WATER-BASED
GLAZING LIQUID**

The dull polished look of sheet metal works well in modern or contemporary homes. While this is an unusual effect, I've used it many times with great success on table-tops and screens, and even on floors. For this faux finish to look authentic, the surface you are transforming must be flat and smooth.

A layer of paste wax is spread over a black base coat, then thick silver-colored glaze is painted over the wax. By scratching off some of the silver-colored glaze to reveal the black base coat, you create the illusion of metal sheets. The wax protects the black base coat. Authentic-looking studs are made by pushing a coin into the wet glaze, removing it, and adding a touch of white highlight. The finished project is a real conversation piece!

Note: Always wear a mask when mixing powdered paint.

PAINT AND TOOLS

BASE COAT:
black latex paint, satin
roller, brush, and paint tray
PAINTED FINISH:
paste wax
silver latex paint or artist's acrylic,
   or silver powder
water-based glazing liquid
mixing container
screwdriver

spatula
roller and paint tray
3" or 4" sponge brushes
thin artist's brush
a small amount of gold artist's
   acrylic paint
a small amount of white latex paint
coin
semigloss varnish

INSTRUCTIONS

For the best results, prepare your surface following the guidelines in the Preparation section (page 42).

Step 1 Base coat: Apply 2 coats of black paint and let dry for 2 to 4 hours.

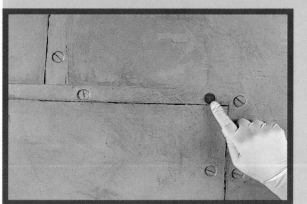

Step 2 Spread a thin coat of wax over the surface with a spatula. Let dry for 2 to 3 hours, depending on the humidity and the thickness of the wax. The wax should be hard.

Step 3 Mix the silver-colored glaze and apply it over the wax coat with a roller.

coin add a little gold paint. Scratch around the imprint and through the middle with a screwdriver, creating a black line.

Step 7 Add white highlights with an artist's brush to one side of the stud. These white marks represent your light source, so paint them along the same side of each stud.

Step 8 Let dry overnight. Finish with 2 coats of semigloss varnish.

Step 4 With a sponge brush, brush out the glaze to create wide, bold linear patterns.

Step 5 With the screwdriver, pull lines through the glaze to create the look of sheets of metal overlapping; be careful not to remove the black base coat.

Step 6 Make the "studs" by pressing a coin into the wet glaze. Remove the coin, and in the indentation left by the

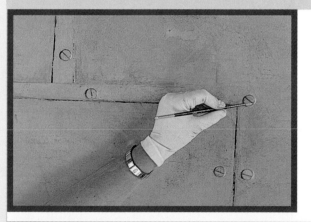

Verdigris

r e c i p e s

For whitewash:
**2 PARTS WHITE LATEX
    PAINT
1 PART WATER**

Verdigris is the effect produced when bronze and copper tarnish over time through oxidation. This weathered finish can be re-created instantly with paint in a color range of blues and greens.

Verdigris can be used on numerous surfaces, indoors and outdoors. New metal, plaster urns, columns, statues, and terra-cotta pots can be beautifully aged. Here, I have applied the verdigris finish to a terra-cotta pot, using a bronze base coat. But if you can't find metallic colors (available at art supply stores), use a burnt orange color simi-lar to that of the terra-cotta pot as the base color. Terra-cotta is very porous, so apply a coat of shellac before you start.

PAINT AND TOOLS

BASE COAT:
bronze or copper acrylic paint, satin
2″ brush
PAINTED FINISH:
a light and a dark shade of blue/
    green latex paint

white latex paint
2″ brush
rags
water spray bottle
matte varnish (optional)

INSTRUCTIONS

If you are working on a terra-cotta or new plaster pot, be sure to seal the surface first with a coat of shellac.

Step 1 Base coat: Apply 1 coat of bronze paint or whatever base coat you have chosen. Let dry.

Step 2 Apply a coat of light blue/green paint and leave it for a few minutes to get tacky.

Step 3 With the water spray bottle, spray the paint at the top of the pot so that the water runs down. The base coat should be revealed in areas as the water eats through the paint.

Step 4 Dab areas of the wet surface with a folded cloth to soften and widen some of the streaks. Let dry.

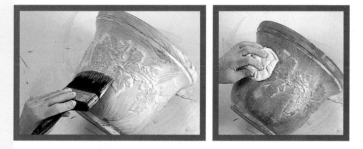

Step 5 Apply the dark blue/green paint over the whole surface, and let it get tacky. Repeat steps 3 and 4 and let dry. You should now have light and dark green patches with streaks of bronze.

Step 6 Mix the whitewash as indicated and brush a small amount of it sparingly onto the surface, getting into any crevices or cracks.

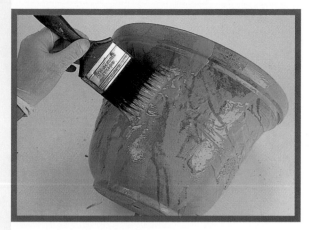

Step 7 With a soft cloth, immediately rub off some of the whitewash and buff the surface, leaving white in the crevices.

Step 8 If the pot is to be used outdoors, apply 2 coats of matte varnish for protection.

ALTERNATIVE

Here a verdigris finish was applied to a round table. To add to the effect, metal lines and bolts were painted on to give the illusion of sheet metal (see page 158 for instructions.) A high-gloss varnish was added for protection and a more contemporary look.

Faux Rust

recipe

1 CUP WATER-BASED
GLAZING LIQUID
1 TABLESPOON
ARTIST'S ACRYLIC
PAINT
2 TABLESPOONS
WATER

You are usually greeted with a smile when you explain that you have gone to the trouble of reproducing rust, since the rest of the population is trying to get rid of it, but it is an ideal finish for fixtures, lamp bases, sconces, or window boxes, and will give cheap metal furniture a more interesting character.

To create this effect, paint is built up in layers and then partially removed with water. Realistic-looking faux rust depends on the random application of the paint so don't worry too much about using smooth, even brush strokes this time. I've used artist's acrylic paints because the colors are more realistic. You only need a small amount for this finish, so why not experiment with the rest?

PAINT AND TOOLS

BASE COAT:
charcoal gray latex paint, satin
PAINTED FINISH:
yellow ochre and red oxide artist's
    acrylic paints
water-based glazing liquid

two 2″ brushes
mixing containers
sea sponge
rag
water spray bottle
matte varnish

Faux Rust

INSTRUCTIONS

For the best results, prepare your surface following the guidelines in the Preparation section (page 42).

Step 1 Base coat: Apply 2 coats of the charcoal gray and let dry 2 to 4 hours.

Step 2 Mix the colored glazes.

Step 3 Apply the red oxide glaze randomly over the surface using a sea sponge to create a mottled effect, leaving 30% of the base color peeking through. Let dry.

Step 4 Holding the softening brush at a right angle to the surface, soften lightly to make a cloudy effect.

Step 5 Spray water over the surface. This will open up the paint to reveal more base coat. Dab with a smooth rag, folded so there are no creases.

Step 6 Sponge on yellow ochre glaze to small areas and soften with a brush. Let dry.

Step 7 When the paint is dry, finish with 1 coat of matte varnish for protection.

NOTE: The rust effect can be varied by playing with the technique until you get the desired results. Just make sure that the paint is applied unevenly.

Gilding

Gilding produces a rich, warm, antique look that is very rewarding to create. The ancient art of gilding is complex and expensive, but today there are simpler, cheaper methods for creating this magical finish. Imitation gold leaf, known as Dutch or composition metal leaf, is available in 4-inch square sheets from art supply and fine paint stores. The leaf is placed over a layer of sticky varnish called gold size. For the cherub on page 167, the surface was previously painted with a red latex paint so that when the gold is rubbed off the gold size, the red base glows through the gold. Start with small projects like lamp bases, plaster molds, and fixtures. Then try large surfaces, or designs on walls, moldings, and furniture. The vestibule on the following page was decorated with gold-leaf stars. The stars were first drawn on the walls, filled in with gold size, and then covered with gold leaf using the same technique as the one used for the cherubs. Gold leaf was also applied to the sconce and mirror.

PAINT AND TOOLS

BASE COAT:
deep red latex paint, flat or satin
paintbrush
PAINTED FINISH:
Gold size, oil- or water-based
Gold leaf (Dutch [composition] metal leaf is the most affordable)

small artist's brush
soft rag
dry brush
varnish—semigloss or high-gloss depending on the look desired
oak stain (optional)

INSTRUCTIONS

For the best results, prepare your surface following the guidelines in the Preparation section (page 42).

Step 1 Base coat: Apply 2 coats of red paint and let dry for 2 to 4 hours.

Step 2 Brush on the gold size over the base coat with a small brush. Cover most of the surface, including the nooks and crannies. Wherever there is gold size, there will be gold. Where there is no gold size, no gold leaf will adhere.

Step 3 Let the gold size dry for approximately 1 hour, until the surface is very tacky to the touch. Hold a sheet of gold leaf in one hand (it's very delicate and will break up easily) and lay it over the tacky surface. With a soft brush, gently brush the gold sheet onto the surface, continuing until the whole area is covered. Let dry completely.

Step 4 The gold size must be dry before the next step. Test by rubbing the surface. If it's still sticky, wait. With a soft brush, dust off the loose bits of gold leaf, exposing the red base coat. Save the little pieces of gold leaf for patching and small projects. If you're afraid you've rubbed off too much in some areas, repeat the process in those areas with more gold size.

Step 5 Polish the surface with a soft rag.

Step 6 Add a clear coat of semi- or high-gloss varnish for protection.

TIPS: Work in a draft-free room.

Be sure your hands are very dry, and don't wear gloves.

The leaf will tear as you brush it onto the tacky surface. Don't worry, just keep applying until you've covered as much of the surface as you wanted to.

ALTERNATIVES

Dutch metal leaf also comes in other metals. Here I've used silver leaf over black artist's acrylic paint. If the gold looks too new, it can be aged by rubbing a little oak stain over the gilded piece before you apply the protective coat of varnish. Or add a bit of stain directly to the varnish.

CHAPTER 8

STENCILING AND BLOCK PAINTING

If you would like more detail on your walls, floors, and furniture, stencils, and block painting can be used to highlight a room, take the place of a molding, or decorate a piece of painted furniture. Both techniques are highly effective, and are similar in that they transfer painted patterns directly onto the surface, but they vary greatly in their execution.

Stenciling is the more common and versatile of the two methods. A stencil is a design that is cut out from a piece of metal, cardboard, plastic, or Mylar. To create the design, you hold the stencil firmly against the surface you want to decorate and fill in the holes with paint. There are literally thousands of designs available, from simple motifs to elaborate architectural details.

In this cheery dining room, a lemon-tree pattern was block painted onto the wall panels, creating a festive setting both for entertaining guests and for family meals.

168

Stenciling

Stenciling is one of the easiest and most inexpensive ways of adding detail and pattern to rooms and furniture. The greatest thing about stenciling is that you don't have to be an artist to paint intricate motifs and designs with a pre-cut stencil, as the difficult work—the designing and cutting—has already been done. All that remains is for you to position the stencil and fill in the holes with paint.

Stencils can be used for decorating most furniture, fixtures, walls, and floors, and are ideal when working with uneven walls and for highlighting arches, beams, doorways, and windows. They're commonly used as a border around a room, but an increasingly popular decorating trend is stenciling repeated patterns all over a wall, which has the look of wall-paper, but is far less expensive.

There are endless designs available in craft and paint stores, and there are specialty stores for stencilers as well as mail-order catalogs, so you will always be able to find a design that suits your needs. Patterns can range from complex to extremely simple, from huge wall designs to tiny motifs used on

Giant stencils were used as a mural on this plain wall.

furniture. Luckily, no matter how complex or simple the stencil, the painting technique is the same. If there is a particular design you are looking for, perhaps to match a fabric pattern, you can always cut your own. Cutting out simple patterns like stars, fish, or geometric shapes is relatively easy, but more complex designs might be difficult to cut precisely. The cost of stencils varies greatly depending on the size and complexity of the design, but with proper care they should last a lifetime. Small rips can be mended with adhesive tape. It's a good idea to start up a collection and share them with friends. And look for a stencil library where you can rent stencils.

Precut Stencils Stencils are made from hard plastic, cardboard, metal, or Mylar.

Cardboard stencils don't last as long as the plastic ones, but they work fine for small areas. Metal stencils are usually used for painting on a flat furniture surface or on paper. Mylar is a high-grade, pliable, transparent plastic sheet, and the stencils cut from Mylar are the most versatile; they are also very strong and easy to clean. Because they are thin and flexible, they wrap easily around corners. The designs in a Mylar stencil are precision-cut using a laser beam, which allows for sharper points and finer pattern definition. Water-based paint can be washed off Mylar stencils with soap and water, and oil-based creams and sticks wipe off with a rag when the painting is completed.

The names of different herbs were stenciled above this kitchen counter.

Designing and Cutting Your Own Stencils If you want to design and cut your own stencil patterns, you can find Mylar in large sheets at craft stores. A simple pattern that fits in with your decor can be copied from fabric or a book. It's best to keep the design as simple as possible, as cutting a complex pattern is difficult. First, enlarge or reduce the design to the size that you require on a photocopy machine. Tape the photocopy to a cutting board, and then tape a piece of Mylar on top. Either trace the pattern with a marker or cut the Mylar out directly over the photocopy using a craft knife. If the design is going to be used as a border, cut small holes as registration marks at either side of the stencil for repositioning. When you are painting or filling in the stencil, add a little paint to this registration mark. This will fit over the next registration mark when the stencil is moved to the right or the left. Wipe off these small marks as you move along the surface. If you are cutting your own stencil, it's a good idea to cut a spare one as a backup.

For a list and full description of the different paints available for stenciling, see pages 35 to 36.

Base Coat for Stenciling You can stencil on most surfaces with the exception of shiny or high-gloss finishes. Do not stencil with water-based paint over an oil base coat. The stencil work will soon scratch off. Although stencils work well on plain surfaces, they really add dimension when applied over painted finishes, in particular

Before you begin, lay out all your materials within easy reach.

colorwashing, ragging, dragging, fresco, and even painted stucco.

Before You Begin Before you start, lay all your tools out. You'll need one stencil brush for each color. It's a good idea to test the stencil on paper or a board. This test sample enables you to check the repeat patterns and the positioning of your design. Tape the sample to the wall or surface you are about to stencil to make sure the height and position are right.

Stenciling Using Liquid Stencil Paint Water-based liquid stencil paints are most commonly used for stenciling, because it's easy to layer colors, several colors can be used at once, and the paint dries very fast. You can use commercial latex paint, following the instructions below, but latex paint does not dry as fast as stencil paint. You only need a tiny

amount and stencil paint comes in small bottles, whereas latex paint comes in larger quantities.

Varnishing Stenciled furniture and floors must be varnished for protection, and a coat of matte varnish should be applied over stenciled wall areas that are likely to be washed and scrubbed like a bathroom or kitchen.

Stenciling Using Creams or Stencil Crayons Stencil crayons (or sticks) and stencil creams are the same; one is compressed into a crayon, the other comes in spill-proof pots. If you are using stencil crayons, remove the protective seal from the tip with a piece of paper towel before you begin. Apply some of the crayon directly onto the Mylar, well away from the cut design, and pick up the paint from there, using a stencil brush. If you are using stencil cream, remove the protective seal from the surface and pick up the paint directly from the pot.

Stenciling Faux Wallpaper Stenciling walls to look like hand-painted wallpaper is currently very fashionable, and looks great! It's a fraction of the cost of real wallpaper, and gives a more subtle look. Choose a motif that works with the theme of your room. The first step is to mark a pattern on the wall where the sten-

cil will go. Use a plumb line, a level, and a ruler or yardstick to make sure the pattern is positioned correctly and spaced evenly. It's a personal choice how close together or far apart to put each stencil design—your eye is the best judge: Too many will look very busy, and too few will lose the impact of the design. Ignore windows, doorframes, and built-in fixtures just as you would if hanging wallpaper or painting stripes. At left, white stars were stenciled over light blue walls, creating a unique pattern. In the middle of each star we pressed an ordinary upholstery tack, also painted white, which makes the pattern three-dimensional, almost exactly like embossed wallpaper.

STENCILING DOS AND DON'TS

Do make sure your surface is clean and dry before you start to stencil.

Don't overload your brush with paint.

Don't stencil on high-gloss surfaces.

Do wash brushes well after completing the project (with paint thinner for creams, crayons, and japan paints; with water for water-based paints such as acrylic and latex).

Do clean the stencil well by soaking it in a paint tray or sink in either water or paint thinner, and then softly wipe off the excess paint.

This pretty stencil pattern was created by first painting the wall yellow and lavender, then applying a leaf stencil in contrasting colors.

Do apply 2 coats of protective varnish in areas that receive considerable wear, for example, on furniture.

Do remember that if you make a mistake, wipe it off immediately using either water or paint thinner and redo that area.

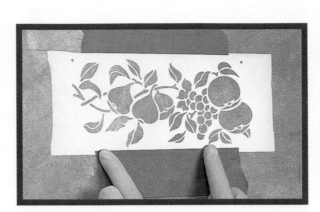

Stenciling

INSTRUCTIONS

Step 1 Lay out your tools before you begin.

Step 2 Mark where the stencil is going to go. Use a pencil so the marks can be erased when the stenciling is completed.

Step 3 Either spray the back of the stencil or use low-tack painter's tape to hold the stencil in place.

Step 4 Dip the stencil brush into the paint and dab off the excess on a paper towel until the brush is almost dry. This is done by swirling the edge of the brush on paper towel. It's important because it prevents the paint from leaking underneath the stencil.

Step 5 Apply the paint to the stencil. You can either pounce the brush up and down over the design or use a circular motion. Work from the edges of the stencil toward the center. Start with a little color and build, adding color and shading.

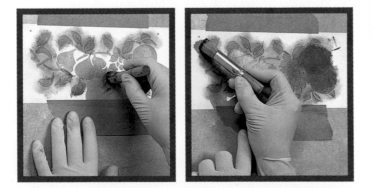

Step 6 Always use a fresh brush for each color.

Step 7 When all colors are on, remove the stencil carefully and make sure there is no paint on the back of the stencil before moving it to the next position. This is done by lining up the repeat markings.

Step 8 When the project is finished, remove pencil marks with an eraser or a small amount of paint thinner.

NOTE: Some stencils come with several layers. Stencil the whole area with the first stencil in the series, and then repeat with the second and sometimes the third stencil overlay. Follow the instructions that are always included with these stencil packs.

Block Painting

Blocking, or block painting, is another old technique that has been enjoying a resurgence of popularity. Traditionally, blocks of wood were carved with intricate patterns, then rolled in paint or dyes, and stamped directly onto walls. Today, the printing blocks are made from soft rubber, and there are a variety of patterns and designs available. They usually take the form of kits that contain several pieces of cut rubber that combine to build up a uniform pattern. Each kit has several pieces centered around a theme, and you build your own design by painting one side of each block with glaze and then pressing it onto the surface. This produces an embossed effect that has a rather unique quality.

Block painting looks fabulous over a painted finish. Colorwashing, fresco, stucco, or ragging are good background choices. If you want to leave your walls plain, then latex paint in a satin finish should be used. You can apply this technique using straight latex paint, but the images will have a more translucent quality if you mix the latex paint with water-based glaze, or use the colored glazes that come with the block painting kits.

PAINT AND TOOLS

latex paint, satin, or skip this
   step if you're applying the pattern
   over a completed painted wall
   finish
BLOCK PAINTING:
blocking kit

water-based paint and water-based
   glazing liquid
or
blocking glaze (available with kits)
½" brushes—1 for each color used
round artist's brush for making vines

INSTRUCTIONS

For information on the blocking kit I've used here, see Resources, page 182.

Step 1 Base coat: Apply 2 coats of latex, or complete a painted finish, and let dry overnight.

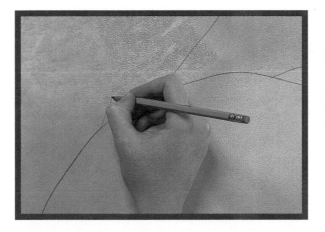

Step 2 Decide where you are going to put the blocking design, and mark with a pencil or masking tape.

Step 3 Hold the leaf block by the tab. Mix colored glaze as indicated. Using a ½″ brush, apply colored glaze to the face of the rubber, either 1 color or a little of both. Make sure the whole surface is covered up to the cut marks at the base of the tab.

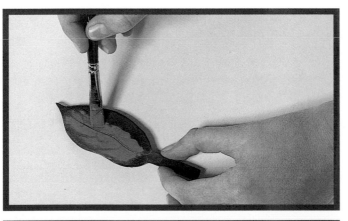

Step 4 Press the pad down firmly on the wall surface and then remove. Press down again; the image will be less bold. The idea is to have some prints stronger than others. Bend pad sideways for half a leaf.

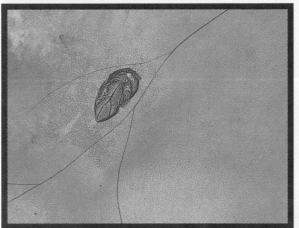

Step 5 After 3 or 4 presses (or different leaves) reapply the glaze and repeat.

Step 6 Block in the leaves first, then the flowers.

Step 7 For vines, pour separate small puddles of clear glaze and green glaze on a plastic plate. Dip the artist's brush into each glaze, keeping colors separate on the brush. Use a pull, twist, and turn motion to make the vines look translucent and natural. Vines should connect leaves, not overlap them.

Step 8 Walls do not need a coat of varnish for protection unless they are in a bathroom or kitchen.

Block Painting

The lemon-tree design on this chair cushion echoes the design on the wall panels in this inviting room.

BLOCK PAINTING ON FABRIC

Block painting looks beautiful on fabric, and the technique is exactly the same as the one used on walls or furniture, you can even use the same kits. Use fabric paint and follow the manufacturer's instructions carefully. Wash, dry, and iron the fabric first, and then tape it down firmly with masking tape. Once you've pressed on the blocks, the paint is permanent, so practice first on some paper until you are pleased with the color and design.

BLOCK PAINTING ON FURNITURE

Block painting on furniture gives the illusion of freehand painting. The technique for block painting is the same as on walls. Make sure the base coat is not high-gloss or oil-based, or your designs will wipe off. When you've finished the block painting, applying one or two coats of varnish for protection.

This fabulous trompe l'oeil bookcase (really a plain armoire) was actually created with a block painting kit. There are four different book spines in the kit, and you can simply apply them to the doors of the armoire following the block painting instructions, but I added an extra step to make the books three-dimensional. First press the blocks onto a sheet of plain paper and cut them out when they're dry. Next take the cardboard center of a paper towel roll, and cut it lengthwise down the middle so that you have two hollow half-moon–shaped pieces. Attach the painted book spines with paper glue and trim off any excess cardboard; then glue them onto the front of the armoire. As the glass was missing from my "bookcase," I glued the spines to pieces of heavy cardboard that were painted dark gray and set them into the spaces where the glass had been. I think it looks terrific!

Resources

United States

CALIFORNIA
Paint Effects San Francisco
2426 Fillmore Street
San Francisco, CA 94115
(415) 292-7780

CONNECTICUT
Art Supply Warehouse
360 Main Avenue (Rte. 7)
Norwalk, CT 06851
(800) 243-5038
(mail-order catalog available)

ILLINOIS
Dick Blick Fine Art Co.
P.O. Box 1267
Galesburg, IL 61401
(800) 447-8192
(mail-order catalog available)

MARYLAND
Duron Paint
call (800) 866-6606 for a dealer
near you.

NEW MEXICO
*Woodworker's Supply of New
Mexico*
5604 Alameda Place NE
Albuquerque, NM 87113
(800) 645-9292
(mail-order catalog available)

NEW YORK
Janovic Plaza
30-35 Thompson Avenue
Long Island City, NY 11101
(718) 786-4444
(mail-order catalog available)

Lee's Art Shop
220 West 57th Street
New York, NY 10019
(212) 247-0110
(mail-order catalog available)

Pearl Paint Company Inc.
308 Canal Street
New York, NY 10013
(800) 221-6845

TEXAS
Texas Art Supply
2001 Montrose
Houston, TX 77006
(713) 526-5221
(mail-order catalog available)

WASHINGTON
Daniel Smith
4128 21st Street
Seattle, WA 98134
(800) 426-6740
(mail-order catalog available)

Canada

ALBERTA
Walls Alive
Call (403) 531-1980 for the
dealer nearest you.
(Alberta)

BRITISH COLUMBIA
Ashley House
Call (604) 734-4130 for the
dealer nearest you.
(Vancouver)

MANITOBA
Living Colour
Call (204) 788-4114 for the
dealer nearest you.
(Winnipeg)

ONTARIO
Bonds Decor
Call (613) 523-1534 for the
dealer nearest you.
(Ottawa)

Home Hardware
Call (519) 664-2252 for the
dealer nearest you.
(across Canada)

Lewiscraft
40 Commander Boulevard
Scarborough, ON
M1S 3S2
(416) 291-8406

White Rose Nurseries
Call (905) 477-3330 for the
dealer nearest you.
(across Canada)

QUEBEC
L'Oiseau Bleu
4146 Ste. Catherine East
Montreal, QC
H1V 1X2
(514) 527-3456

Montreal Decorators
250 Ste. Catherine East
Montreal, QC
H2X 1L5
(800) 215-6910

Ro-na Hardware
call (514) 599-5100 for the
dealer nearest you.
(across Quebec)

Martin & Associates
In Canada, call (800) 204-6278
for the dealer nearest you.
(Montreal and Toronto)

Savoir-Faire
In the United States, call (800)
332-4660 for the dealer
nearest you.
(California)

All stencils in this book were
designed by
The Stencil Library
Stocksfield Hall
Stocksfield, Northumberland
NE43 7TN England

Backstreet
3905 Steve Reynolds Boulevard
Norcross, GA 30093
(770) 381-7373

Cutbill & Company Ltd.
274 Sherman Avenue N
Unit 207
Hamilton, ON L8L 6N6
(905) 547-8525

*Homestead House Paint
Company*
In Canada, call (416) 504-9984
for the dealer nearest you.
(color brochure available)

Old Village
In the United States, call (800)
498-7687 for the dealer
nearest you.

Index

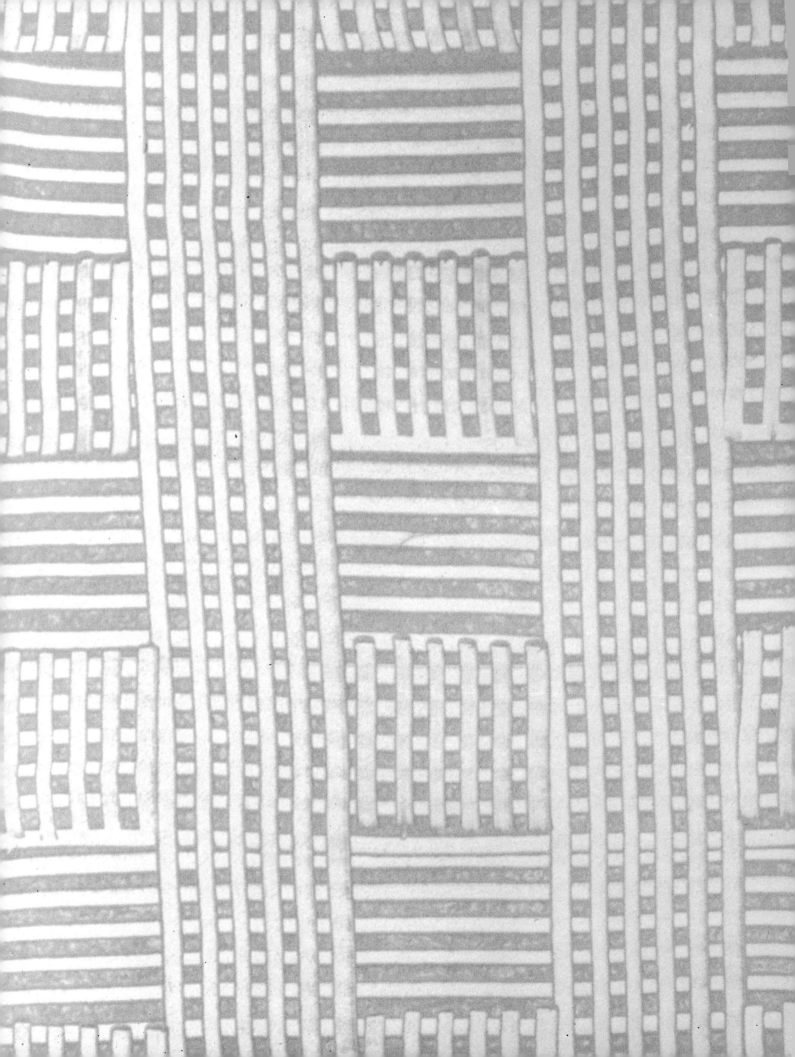